THE RIGHT WAY TO READ MUSIC

Harry and Michael Baxter

RIGHT WAY

Typeset in 10½/11½pt Times by County Typesetters, Margate, Kent.

Music typeset by Halstan & Co. Ltd, Amersham, Buckinghamshire.

Printed and bound in Great Britain by Cox & Wyman Ltd., Reading, Berkshire.

The *Right Way* series is published by Elliot Right Way Books, Brighton Road, Lower Kingswood, Tadworth, Surrey, KT20 6TD, U.K. For information about our company and the other books we publish, visit our web site at www.right-way.co.uk

DEDICATION

The authors of this book wish to acknowledge the editorial work done by Miss Melanie Rae, whose experience in the world of publishing and formerly as Head of Music at her school has, we believe, helped us to make the book very suitable for students, the private teacher and for use in schools.

AUTHORS' NOTE

The purpose of this book is to bring an understanding of the subject of music theory to students and lovers of music. With this aim in mind, and to help you gauge your progress, there are sets of questions at the end of each chapter, to test how much you have understood of the material contained within it. These should be answered in a separate music manuscript book, parts of questions being copied out as necessary.

CONTENTS

1

PITCH

Music is concerned with sound – but only some sounds. Some sounds are very heavy and deep; others are light and high. All sounds are caused by something vibrating, that is, a small to and fro movement. Sometimes the movement is so fast that we cannot hear it – a very high sound, for instance, like a dog whistle. If we hear a very low note on an organ, sometimes, we can actually feel the floor moving. We call the height or depth of a sound its pitch.

If we look at the notes on a piano we will see that there are more than eighty. We do not invent a different name for each note but use seven, and keep repeating them from A to G. A.B.C.D.E.F.G., A.B.C.D.E.F.G., A.B.C.D.E.F.G., etc.

To show these sounds on paper we use a set of five lines with four spaces between. This is called a stave or staff.

Each line and each space represents a note. The name of the note is determined by the type of clef that appears at the beginning of the stave.

Treble Clef

The treble clef is used for high notes. It is sometimes called the G clef because it curls round the line that represents the note G.

Now we can work out the names of all the other lines and spaces.

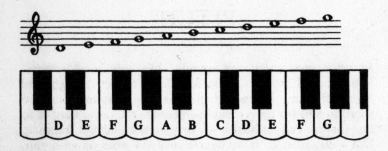

Bass Clef

To write notes for the low sounds we use the bass clef. This clef is sometimes called the F clef since it loops round this line on the stave, and the dots go either side of this line.

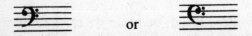

or

The notes on these lines and spaces are as follows:

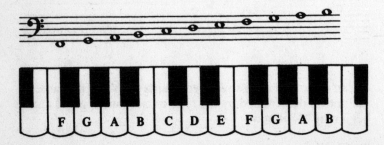

Some notes have to be written above or below the stave and short lines, called leger lines, have to be used to extend the range of the stave.

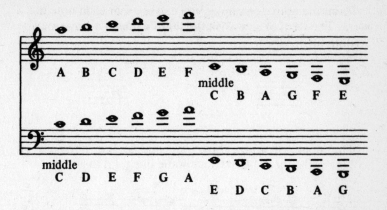

To prevent too many leger lines being used the sign 8 or 8va is written above or below the music followed by a dotted or continuous line. The sign stops working when a bracket ⌐——————— or ———————⌐ occurs at the end. The sign represents ottava, the Italian word for octave.

From the above examples you can see that each note has a stem. The stem of a note on the middle line of a stave may be written up or down:

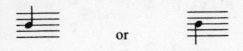

The stems of notes above the middle line normally go down, whilst those below the middle line tend to go up:

Piano music uses 2 staves bracketed together. The music in the top stave is usually played by the right hand and uses notes in the treble clef, whilst the bottom stave is played by the left hand since music for the bass clef is written on this stave. The 2 staves are joined together by the note middle C.

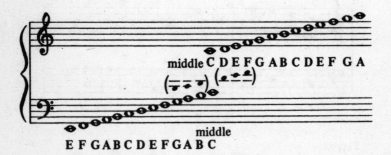

Other Clefs
There are other important clefs. The first, called the tenor clef, is often found in cello, bassoon and tenor trombone music and allows the full range of these instruments to be exploited without using too many leger lines.

 middle C

The second clef is the alto clef and is used by the viola.

 middle C

In both cases the line that passes through the two arms is middle C. It is for this reason that both these clefs are occasionally referred to as the C clefs.

QUESTIONS

1. (a) How many different letter names do we use to determine the notes?
   (b) What are the letter names?
   (c) What do we do when we reach the letter G?

2. (a) How many lines do we use to write notes?
   (b) How many spaces do we use?
   (c) What are the sets of lines and spaces called?

3. What is the name that we give to the sign which tells us the names of the notes?

4. What two names do we use for the sign to name notes in the treble range?

5. Draw the correct sign, identified in question 4, at the beginning of a set of five lines and write in the names given to notes on each line and space.

6. (a) What is the name of the note below D?
    (b) What is the name of the note above F?
    (c) Where is the note C always to be found on the piano keyboard?
    (d) Where is the note F always to be found on the piano keyboard?

7. What do we call the clef we use when writing low sounds?

8. Write out, on a stave, the clef we use for low sounds. Then write the notes E and Middle C in an appropriate position and A in two positions.

9. (a) Why do we call Middle C by this name?
    (b) Choosing the correct clef, write:
        (i) the note Middle C above a stave
        (ii) the note A above a stave.

10. (a) What is a leger line?
    (b) When do we use a leger line?
    (c) If lots of notes requiring leger lines are needed what alternative to leger lines is there?

11. (a) On a stave draw:
        (i) the alto clef and the note Middle C
        (ii) the tenor clef and the note Middle C.
    (b) Which instruments use these clefs?
    (c) By what other name are these clefs sometimes referred?

2

RHYTHM

We have learned that sounds can be high or low. We know
from listening to music that it can be loud or soft. We also
know that some sounds are long and others short. In music,
when we speak of the length of sound, we usually mean how
many beats it contains. Music is made up from beats; and
beats are made up from notes of different lengths.

If we listen to a waterfall we hear one continuous sound
without any regular beat. If we listen to a leaky tap we hear
the regular beat of the dripping water. Or, if we listen to the
sound of the wheels while on a train journey, we shall find
that when travelling at a steady speed there is a definite
throb, the evenness of which might well send us to sleep.

We can make up all kinds of counting to fit the time of the
water dripping from the leaky tap or from a roof or window
sill. We cannot make any beats or rhythms from the sound of
the waterfall, or from any sounds which are continuous. The
sounds from the wheels of a moving train are continuous but
not steady – there is a throb, a beat. Sometimes they seem to
be saying things to us. We hear la-la-la-la; la-la-la-la. They
could be saying 'nearly home now; nearly home now'.
Sometimes they seem to say la-di-da; la-di-da, or 'back to
school, back to school'.

Note Values
In music we can recognise the lengths of different notes by
their shapes, by whether they have stems or stems and tails,
or by whether they are just circles or are filled in and are
black. Each note (which shows a sound) has its equivalent
sign, called a rest (which shows a silence) to correspond in
value.

Here is a list of all the notes we use in music. We start with a circle, add lines called stems, fill in the head of the note and add more lines called tails. Of course, at first, we should use only a few of these notes and work up to using the others, gradually. Be careful to learn the rests as well as the notes. The most common single-beat note or rest we use is called a crotchet. The following table shows the value of each note and rest as a multiple or fraction of a crotchet.

Note (Sound)	Name	Value	Rest (Silence)
‖o‖	Breve	8	
o	Semibreve	4	i.e. it hangs from the 2nd line down
♩ or ⌐	Minim	2	i.e. it sits on the middle line
♩ or ⌐	Crotchet	1	⌐ or ⌐ (second used in printed music)
♪ or ♪	Quaver	½	
♪ or ♪	Semiquaver	¼	
♪ or ♪	Demisemiquaver	⅛	
♪ or ♪	Hemidemisemiquaver	$\frac{1}{16}$	

When writing these notes we must remember that the stem is written upwards if the note is below the middle line, and downwards if the note is above the middle line. If the note is on the middle line the stem may be written either upwards or downwards.

The tail of a note for a quaver beat, or smaller value note, is always written on the right of the stem.

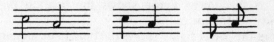

When we use quavers we nearly always join them in pairs. This is because a lot of music has crotchet beats: there are two quavers in each crotchet beat, and we always group notes into beats. The quavers are joined at the end of the stems. A single quaver is ♪ or ♪ but a pair of quavers (making a crotchet) is ♫ or ♫ . Similarly semiquavers (having two tails) are joined by two lines, and so on.

Time Signatures

Some clocks and watches make a regular sound, often at sixty ticks every minute. This is a very fine way to understand what these notes can be made to mean. Counting 'tick tock' suggests beats in two. A loud ONE and a soft two and three makes beats in threes. Using groups of four ticks suggests beats in fours. The even beat of the clock allows all sorts of variations.

When soldiers march, 'left, right' keeps them in step. Shouting 'one, two' would have the same effect. This is a good example of an even beat.

You will see that the longest note we use is a breve. It is twice as long as a semibreve. If we think of a breve lasting, or being worth, eight beats, a semibreve will be worth four beats. A minim note will be worth only two beats, and a crotchet just one beat.

Lines drawn across the stave divide the music into bars. These divide the music into equal parts, each bar having the same number of beats as all the others in the music.

To make plain how many beats a composer wants in each bar, and what each beat is worth, two figures are written,

one above the other, at the beginning of the music. The
upper figure states how many beats in each bar. The lower
figure tells us what each beat is worth. These figures are
called the *time signature*.

Because the breve is very seldom used, the semibreve may
be regarded as the whole note. The lower figure of the time
signature states what part of a semibreve, or whole note, is
the beat.

Two as this lower figure shows the beat to be half a
semibreve – a minim.

Four as the lower figure shows the beat to be a quarter of a
semibreve – a crotchet.

Eight as the lower figure shows the beat to be an eighth of
a semibreve – a quaver; and so on.

Two beats in each bar,
each being a crotchet.

Three beats in each bar,
each being a crotchet.

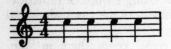

Four beats in each bar,
each being a crotchet.

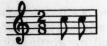

Two beats in each bar,
each being a quaver.

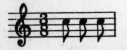

Three beats in each bar,
each being a quaver.

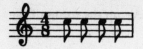 Four beats in each bar,
each being a quaver.

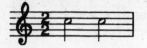 Two beats in each bar,
each being a minim.

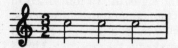 Three beats in each bar,
each being a minim.

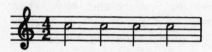 Four beats in each bar,
each being a minim.

All these time signatures have two numbers. The lower number of all these time signatures have shown beats we can divide by two or four or eight. Minim beats = two crotchets, four quavers, etc. These time signatures are called simple time signatures.

Sometimes, we use a capital C to show four crotchet beats in each bar. $\frac{4}{4}$ is the most commonly used time signature and is known as Common Time. When the beats are to be minims, sometimes we use ¢, but this does not tell us how many beats to the bar.

So, C = $\frac{4}{4}$

¢ = Minim beats: either $\frac{2}{2}$ or $\frac{4}{2}$.

The sign ¢ is called Alla Breve because originally this sign was used to show that the beat was the breve rather than the semibreve. Today it tells us that the beat is a minim rather than the more usual crotchet.

Notes of less value than a crotchet must always be grouped together to show the value of the beat. We do this by joining them at the end of the stem.

Rests
Notes less in value than the beat and followed by a silence (a

rest) must have a rest, or rests, to make up the value of the beat.

In the first bar we have the time signature of four beats in the bar, each being a crotchet. Then come four single beats. In the second bar we have a rest. This is a quaver rest so it needs the value of half a beat to make up the crotchet. This is done by making the first note in this bar a quaver. In the last bar, the two quavers make the first crotchet beat. Then comes a quaver note followed by a quaver rest, making up the second beat. Finally, the minim makes up the last two beats.

Remember that the numbers must be even and steady. You will notice that, in order to fit a sound between the four numbered beats above, we have used an '&' (and). This '&' fits exactly between the two numbers. Imagine the ticking of a clock relentlessly fitting the numbers you are counting.

It is also possible to use one note or rest for several beats where we might have used several notes. For example:

If we wanted silence for beats three and four in the first bar we would write a minim rest (two beats) and not two crotchet rests.

If we wanted a single long note at the beginning we might write a minim.

We can generally write a two beat rest (or note) at the beginning of a bar but rarely anywhere else. In $\frac{4}{4}$ time, a two beat rest can be on beats one and two or three and four, but *never* on beats two and three and this must be considered a dangerous practice for examinations.

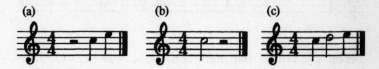

(a) and (b) are correct; (c) is wrong and should be written using two crotchet notes. The reason for not being able to use a minim in $\frac{4}{4}$ time on beats two and three is that it should always be possible to draw an imaginary line down the middle of the bar.

It is safer not to write the pattern from (c) above but to use a tie to join the two crotchet notes as a single sound. A tie is a curved line,

joining the two notes into a single sound lasting their joint value.

A tie cannot be used to join rests in the same way: rests are silence, and silence only ends when a sound occurs and is therefore continuous until interrupted!

Some beats are accented: they are louder than other beats

and are called strong beats. The other beats of the bar are weak beats. Most music has the first beat of a bar accented for, without this throb or accent, such music does not make rhythmic sense.

In triple time (three beats in the bar), the first beat of the bar is strong and the other two weak. In duple time (two beats in the bar) the first of the bar is strong and the second weak. In quadruple time (four beats in the bar) the first of the bar is strong, the second weak, the third medium and the last weak.

You will notice that there is a double bar line whenever the time signature is changed. One can use a double bar line anywhere, to show a change in the music, or at the end of the section. Normally, however, it is used at the end of a section or at the conclusion of the music. A double bar line in the middle of the music looks like

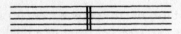

but at the conclusion of music the second line is thicker, and looks like

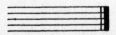

Dotted Notes
Both notes and rests may be lengthened by adding, immediately afterwards, a dot, or dots.

One dot lengthens the sound (note) or silence (rest) by half the value of the original note or rest. So, a dotted semibreve is worth six crotchets. A dotted minim is worth three crotchets. A dotted crotchet is worth three quavers, and so on.

If we add two dots after a note, or rest, the sound, or silence, is lengthened by an extra quarter of the value of the original note or rest. In other words, a second dot adds half the value of the first dot.

QUESTIONS

1. What do we mean by the length of a sound?

2. What does the word 'beat' mean?

3. (a) How do we show the different lengths of notes?
    (b) What does a rest mean?

4. Write each of the following notes or rests:
    a semibreve note   a minim note   a quaver rest
    a crotchet note   a crotchet rest

5. If a breve lasts eight beats:
    (i)   how many beats would a crotchet be worth?

(ii)   how many beats would a minim be worth?
(iii)   how many beats would a semibreve be worth?

6.   What is a bar line and why is it used?

7.   (a)   What is a time signature?
      (b)   What does the upper figure tell us?
      (c)   What does the lower figure tell us?
      (d)   If the lower figure is a 2, what does this mean?
      (e)   Explain the following: $\frac{2}{3}$; $\frac{4}{2}$; $\frac{8}{3}$.
      (f)   What is a simple time signature?
      (g)   Give three examples of a simple time signature.

8.   (a)   What does the time signature **C** mean?
      (b)   What does **C** mean?
      (c)   What name do we give to the sign **¢** and when is it used?

9.   Correct this:

10.   Add rests as necessary to complete these bars.

11.   (a)   What does the word accented mean?
      (b)   Where do we usually find an accented beat?

12. Where do strong and weak beats occur in the following times?
    (i)   quadruple time;
    (ii) triple time;
    (iii) duple time.

13. Show which beats are strong, medium and weak in the following bars.

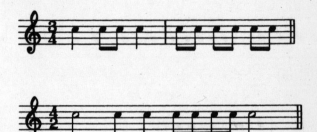

14. (a) What is a double bar line?
    (b) When do we use one?

15. Here is the tune of 'Twinkle, twinkle little star'. Rewrite it with the correct rhythm. You need use only crotchets and minims. The time signature should be $\frac{2}{4}$. Put in the bar lines.

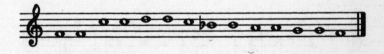

16. Write out this tune and underneath write the numbers you would count in order to clap it.

17.   Learn to clap the following rhythms, counting aloud as necessary.

(i)

(ii)

(iii)

18.   Write this out correctly.

19.   Complete these bars with correct rests where starred.

20.   Complete these bars with rests correctly grouped.

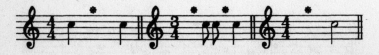

21. Complete these bars with notes correctly grouped.

22. Write these correctly:

(i)

(ii)

23. (a) What happens when we add a dot after a note?
    (b) How many crotchets equal a dotted minim in length?
    (c) Write out the following in full:

24. Put bar lines into the following:

(i)

(ii)

(iii)

(iv)

3

MORE ABOUT NOTATION

Accidentals

The keys on the piano are arranged in a pattern of black and white notes. Black notes take their names from the white notes. A black note to the right of a white note is higher in pitch and is identified by the white letter name plus the word 'sharp'. Similarly, a black note to the left of a white note is lower in pitch and is identified by the white letter name plus the word 'flat'.

The same process can be applied to any note next to a white note, even another white note!

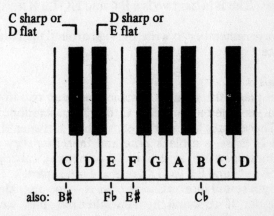

Therefore, every black or white note has two names. The musical sign for a sharp is ♯ and the sign for a flat is ♭ . They always appear before the note when written on a stave (see over), but after the letter name of the note when it is written elsewhere.

To cancel the sharp or flat a natural sign is used ♮.

Sharps, flats and naturals are called *accidentals* and the effect of an accidental applies only to the note before which it is written, whenever it appears at that pitch *in that bar*. It does not affect notes at any other octave and is cancelled by a bar line.

The B in bar two is a B ♮ and NOT a B ♭.

Always remember to write the sign around the correct line or space.

Intervals

On the piano the smallest distance between two notes (i.e. interval) is called a semitone. C to C♯ is a semitone, so is E to F. These notes are next to each other. Between the notes C and D there is a black note and therefore they are two semitones apart or as it is more commonly called, a tone apart. F to G and F♯ to G♯ are also a tone apart.

We can sound intervals in two ways – one after the other, or together. If we sound them one after the other, we make a melody, so this way is called melodic; and if we sound intervals together we make a chord or harmony, so this way is called harmonic.

There are two kinds of semitone; that retaining the same letter name, like C to C♯, called a Chromatic semitone, and that having a different letter name, like C to D♭, called a Diatonic semitone.

We use numbers to identify intervals. For instance, C to D is a 2nd because two consecutive letters are involved. C to E is a 3rd because three letters are used (C, D, E).

Accidentals do not alter the number or the alphabetical part of the interval. D to F is always a 3rd, whatever sharps or flats are added to either letter. D to F, D♭ to F, D to F♯ and so on are all 3rds. The accidentals merely alter the *type* of interval. There are five names for the different types of interval. These names are:

Major	– 2nds, 3rds, 6ths and 7ths;
Minor	– major intervals made a chromatic semitone smaller;
Perfect	– 4ths, 5ths and 8ths (or octave);
Diminished	– minor or perfect intervals made a chromatic semitone smaller;
Augmented	– major or perfect intervals made a chromatic semitone larger.

The Scale

If we write a ladder of notes, each having a different letter name, we create a scale. The scale of C has the notes C, D, E, F, G, A, B and C. Note that we end on the same letter name as the one with which we started, but eight notes higher. This space of eight notes we call an octave.

If we write out the scale of C we find C to D is a tone, D to E is a tone, E to F is a semitone, F to G is a tone, G to A is a tone, A to B is a tone and B to C is a semitone. This makes up the scale of C major. All major scales have the pattern tone, tone, semitone, tone, tone, tone, semitone (usually written TTS, TTTS) between the notes.

If we work out a major scale on a keyboard starting on a note other than C we must use black notes. We can now work out the notes of the scales starting on G and D, remembering to use the pattern TTS, TTTS.

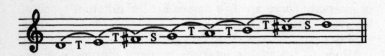

Let us examine the intervals within the C major scale.

     C to D is a major 2nd.
     C to E is a major 3rd.
     C to F is a perfect 4th.
     C to G is a perfect 5th.
     C to A is a major 6th.
     C to B is a major 7th.
     C to C is a perfect octave, or unison.

It will be seen that intervals in a major scale are either major or perfect, according to their numerical value. It is the major scale we use as a basis from which to identify the type of interval.

More Accidentals

We have learned that the sharp, flat, or natural each alter a note by one semitone. When we want to alter a note by a tone, we use a double sharp or a double flat.

A double sharp raises a note by two semitones (a tone). The sign used is ✖.

This note 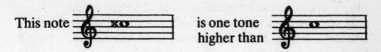 is one tone higher than

A double flat lowers a note by two semitones (a tone). It is written as two flats (𝄫), together before the note even when the key signature has flats in it.

The note 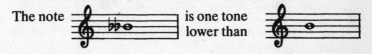 is one tone lower than

To cancel either the double sharp or double flat and restore the note to its original pitch we need to write a natural sign (to cancel the first sharp or flat) and a single sharp or flat (see page 56). To cancel a double accidental and remove both sharps or both flats two natural signs would have to be used.

Already, we have found several examples of one sound having two names. For instance, C♯ has the same sound as D♭, F♯ the same sound as G♭, and so on. If we study the diagram below we shall see that there are three names for every note except A♭. It is not necessary to learn all these names but we must be able to work them out when needed.

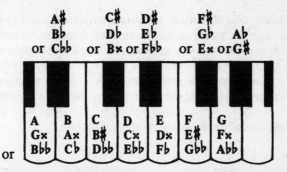

This change in name only is called enharmonic. So, enharmonic means giving a note or notes different names without changing the actual pitch.

Augmented and Diminished Intervals

Major intervals can be made smaller or larger in size.

If we reduce a major interval by a chromatic semitone it becomes minor. C to E, a major 3rd, reduced to C to E♭ becomes a minor 3rd.

If we further reduce the minor interval to C to E♭♭ we produce a diminished 3rd.

If we increase the major 3rd C to E by one chromatic semitone to C to E♯, we produce an augmented 3rd.

So: major, one chromatic semitone smaller, becomes minor;
minor, one chromatic semitone smaller, becomes diminished;
perfect, one chromatic semitone smaller, becomes diminished;
major, one chromatic semitone larger, becomes augmented;
minor, one chromatic semitone larger, becomes major;
perfect, one chromatic semitone larger, becomes augmented.

A graphical explanation of this might be:

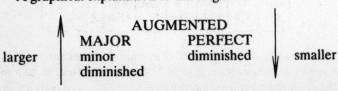

There are six semitones in a diminished 5th, and there are six semitones in an augmented 4th. Six half tones are the same as three full tones, and we call the intervals of a diminished 5th and an augmented 4th by the name *tritone* (tri – meaning three, like triangle or tricycle). A tritone is exactly half an octave.

Inversions
We can invert intervals by making the lower note the higher.

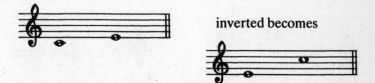

inverted becomes

This produces quite a different kind of interval.
   Thus: major intervals become minor
          minor intervals become major
          augmented intervals become diminished
          perfect intervals remain perfect
          diminished intervals become augmented.
The sounds produced by intervals are either concords or discords.
Concords can either be perfect or imperfect. Imperfect concords are the major and minor 3rd and 6th and perfect concords are the perfect 4th, 5th and octave.
Any other intervals are discords.
The most important fact to remember about intervals concerns their size. Because the numerical size of an interval is determined by the number of letter names between the lower and upper notes we cannot alter the numerical part of its description, whatever accidentals are involved, unless we change the alphabetic name of one note. Thus,

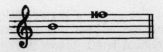

remains some kind of 5th because there are five letter names involved. The fact that the F𝗑 is enharmonically also the note G, does not make this interval a 6th. If we invert it, of course, it becomes a 4th, because between any kind of F and any kind of B there are four alphabetical letters.

We *always* work out intervals *upwards*. When we need to find an interval below a certain note, it is best to invert the interval and then write the new note an octave lower. For example, a minor 3rd below A is the same as a major 6th above, that is, F♯.

If the lower note of any interval is not the tonic (see below) of a major scale, an enharmonic change of both notes may help. A 6th above G♯ is enharmonically the same as a 6th above A♭. So, a major 6th above G♯ has to be some kind of E. There is no major key of G♯ (see *Key Signatures*, page 42), so we will think of G♯ being A♭ and a major 6th above A♭ is F. We must make this some sort of E – so it must be E♯.

Enharmonically the same notes

Ab = G♯
F = E♯

Another way uses the major scale, starting on the white note of a keyboard, with sharps or flats. For example, to find the interval C𝗑 to B: in the C major scale, C to B is a major 7th; C♯ to B is one semitone smaller – a minor 7th; C𝗑 is one semitone smaller still – a diminished 7th.

Technical Names of Notes

Each note or degree of a major scale has a different letter name. This means that it is a diatonic scale. Apart from the alphabetical letter names of notes, every degree of a diatonic scale has a technical name. The first (the key note) is called the *tonic*; the second, the *supertonic*; the third, the *mediant*; the fourth, the *subdominant*; the fifth, the *dominant*; the sixth, the *submediant*; the seventh, the *leading note*; and the eighth, the *tonic*, again.

It may help to remember these names in this way:

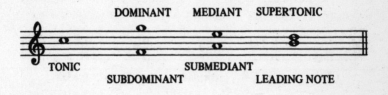

The dominant is a 5th above the tonic, whilst the subdominant is a 5th below the tonic, hence the use of the prefix 'sub'. Similarly the mediant is a 3rd above the tonic, and the submediant is a 3rd below.

Supertonic (super meaning *above*), means above the tonic by one note. Leading note leads us home to the tonic.

QUESTIONS

1. What is an accidental?

2. Does an accidental alter any note except the one in front of which it is written?

3. (a) What does a natural look like?
   (b) When do we use a natural?
   (c) What does a flat do to a note?
   (d) What does a sharp do to a note?

4. How long does the effect of a sharp, flat or natural last?

5.   From the following list write out
     (i)   the letter names that are a tone apart
     (ii) the letter names that are a semitone apart:
     C to D   D to E   E to F   F to G
     G to A   A to B   B to C.

6.   (a)   Which of the following notes have the correct
           names?

(i) E♭   (ii) C♯   (iii) G♯   (iv) B♭   (v) D♭

(b)   Raise or lower these notes by a semitone, using
      the correct accidental.

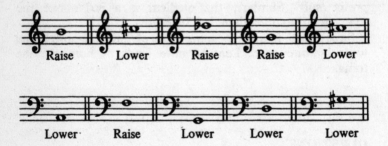

7.   (a)   Would the note marked with an asterisk be B♭
           or B♮? Why?

(b)   Would the note marked with an asterisk be F♯
      or F♮? Why?

8. (a) What is a melodic interval?
    (b) What is a harmonic interval?

9. (a) What is a chromatic semitone?
    (b) What is a diatonic semitone?
    (c) Show which of these are chromatic semitones:

10. What number describes each of these intervals:
     C to E;   D to A;   F to D;   G to A;   C to B?

11. (a) Do accidentals alter the number part of an
         interval?
     (b) How does an accidental affect an interval?

12. How would you describe the following intervals?
     (i)   2nds, 3rds, 6ths, 7ths
     (ii) Major intervals made one chromatic semitone
          smaller
     (iii) 4ths, 5ths, 8ths or octaves
     (iv) Minor or perfect intervals made a chromatic
          semitone smaller
     (v)   Major or perfect intervals made a chromatic
          semitone larger.

13. What is the sign for a double sharp, and what does it
     mean?

14. What is the sign for a double flat, and what does it
     mean?

15. (a) What is an enharmonic change?

(b) Change the following notes enharmonically. There are two changes to each note.

(i)   (ii)   (iii)

(iv)   (v)   (vi)

16. In what way can we alter major intervals?

17. By how much do we reduce a major interval to make it minor?

18. Explain how a major interval may be made into a diminished one.

19. Explain how a major interval may be made into an augmented one.

20. (a) Why is E to F a minor 2nd?
    (b) Why is B to C a minor 2nd?
    (c) Why is D to F a minor 3rd?
    (d) Why is E to G a minor 3rd?
    (e) Why is F to B an augmented 4th?
    (f) Why is B to F a diminished 5th?

21. (a) How many semitones are there in the intervals of a diminished 5th and an augmented 4th?
    (b) What other name describes the diminished 5th and the augmented 4th?

22. How do we invert intervals?

23. What do these intervals become when inverted?
    diminished   major   minor
    augmented   perfect.

24. Complete the sentence: "The sounds produced by intervals are either . . . . . or . . . . ."

25. (a) What two descriptions do we give to concords?
    (b) Describe each type of concord.

26. What are discords?

27. What is the important fact to remember about intervals?

28. What are the intervals drawn below?

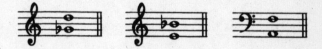

29. (a) Write the following intervals in the treble clef:
    (i)   Perfect 4th above E ♭
    (ii)   Major 7th above C ♯
    (iii) Minor 3rd below A ♭.
    (b) Write the following intervals in the bass clef:
    (i)   Major 2nd above F ♯
    (ii)   Diminished 7th below D
    (iii) Augmented 4th above F.

30. Write the names of these intervals:

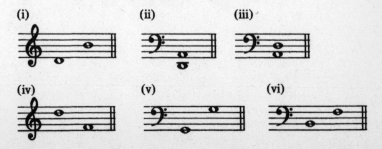

31. (a) What is a scale?
    (b) What are the notes of the scale of C?
    (c) What is an octave?
    (d) What does the word 'diatonic' mean?

32. (a) What is a tone?
    (b) What is a semitone?
    (c) What is the pattern of tones and semitones in a major scale?

33. (a) Write out, in the correct order, the technical names given to each degree of the scale.
    (b) How do we always count the degrees of the scale – upwards or downwards?

4

SCALES AND KEYS

Major Scale
Every major scale is made up from two halves. The C scale has C, D, E, F and G, A, B, C. Each half is called a *tetrachord* and is made up by a tone, a tone and a semitone. There is a tone linking the two tetrachords (F to G). All major scales can be divided into these two halves.

In C major, the upper tetrachord is G, A, B, C. These notes make up the lower tetrachord of G major. The upper tetrachord of G major (D, E, F♯, G) is the lower tetrachord of D major. This change always happens when we add one sharp more to the new signature. *Remember that in sharp keys, the upper tetrachord becomes the lower tetrachord of the key with one extra sharp*. Therefore, the lowest note of the upper tetrachord of the old key becomes the tonic, or keynote, of our new sharp key.

The seventh note of a major scale is always one semitone below the keynote. In G major, for instance, the keynote is G, the seventh (F♯) is one semitone below G. This seventh

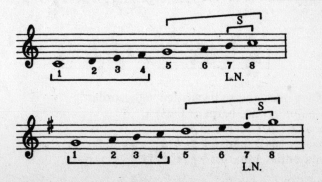

41

note leads the ear to return to the key note and is, therefore, called a *leading note* (L.N.).

Key Signatures
We could write all our music by using an accidental in front of every note we wanted to alter, but this would make our music very difficult to read. So, we collect our sharps or flats together and write them only at the beginning of every line. This, we call a key signature.

A key signature is either made up of sharps or of flats, never a mixture of both.

If a key signature is changed in a piece of music a double bar line occurs, followed by the new key signature.

To create the key with one more sharp than the present key the following process should be adopted:

1. The new scale starts on the fifth degree of the previous scale.
2. The notes of this new scale will be the same as in the old scale, but the penultimate note must be a semitone below the keynote, and will need a sharp to be added to the key signature.

Thus an order of sharps emerges: F♯, C♯, G♯, D♯, A♯, E♯, B♯.

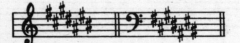

They must always be written in this order:
(C major has no sharps or flats)
G major has 1 sharp : F♯
D major has 2 sharps: F♯, C♯
A major has 3 sharps: F♯, C♯, G♯

E major has 4 sharps: F♯, C♯, G♯, D♯
B major has 5 sharps: F♯, C♯, G♯, D♯, A♯
F♯ major has 6 sharps: F♯, C♯, G♯, D♯, A♯, E♯
C♯ major has 7 sharps: F♯, C♯, G♯, D♯, A♯, E♯, B♯.

Here are the major scales with up to four sharps.

E Major

A similar pattern emerges with key signatures that are made up of flats.

In C major, the lower tetrachord is C, D, E, F. This is also the upper tetrachord of F major, which key has one flat. The lower tetrachord of F major (F, G, A, B♭) is also the upper tetrachord of B flat major, which key has two flats. *Remember that in flat keys, the lower tetrachord becomes the upper tetrachord of the key with one extra flat.* Therefore, the highest note of the lower tetrachord of the old key becomes the tonic, or keynote, of our new flat key.

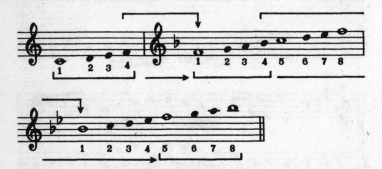

Just as key signatures with sharps had a pattern, those with flats do as well. The difference is that each new flat added is a fourth away from the previous one: B♭, E♭, A♭, D♭, G♭, C♭, F♭.

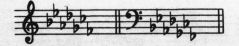

F major has 1 flat: B♭
B♭ major has 2 flats: B♭, E♭

E♭ major has 3 flats: B♭, E♭, A♭
A♭ major has 4 flats: B♭, E♭, A♭, D♭
D♭ major has 5 flats: B♭, E♭, A♭, D♭, G♭
G♭ major has 6 flats: B♭, E♭, A♭, D♭, G♭, C♭
C♭ major has 7 flats: B♭, E♭, A♭, D♭, G♭, C♭, F♭

Here are the major scales with up to four flats.

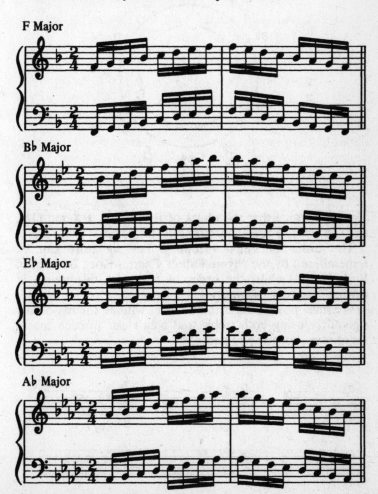

A useful way of remembering the order of the sharp and flat keys is as follows. Clockwise gives the sharp keys, by counting up a fifth for each new key, and anticlockwise the flat keys by counting up a fourth between each new key.

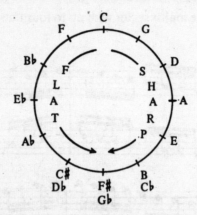

You will notice that the scales of B and C♭, F♯ and G♭, and C♯ and D♭ are enharmonically the same.

The order of sharps within a key signature can be remembered by the rhyme **Father Charles Goes Down And Ends Battle**, whilst the order of flats uses this rhyme in reverse (see pages 42 and 44).

We must now familiarise ourselves with all the major key signatures using both treble and bass clefs. In each case a semibreve shows the key note.

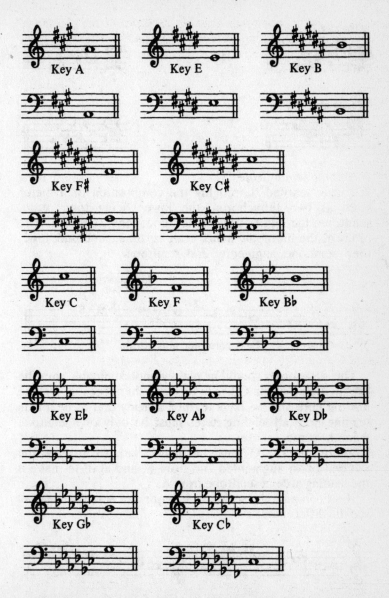

We must also learn the positions on the stave for the sharps and flats when we use a key signature with the Alto or Tenor clefs.

Alto clef

Tenor clef

Harmonic Minor Scale

We have learned thoroughly the composition of a major scale as two tetrachords, the lower being tone, tone, semitone; the higher being tone, tone, tone, semitone. The order of the harmonic minor scale is: tone, semitone, tone, tone, semitone, augmented 2nd, semitone.

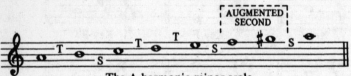

The A harmonic minor scale

This scale order should be plainly understandable with the explanation that the G has to be made sharp because it is the leading note and we have learned already that to be a true leading note all leading notes must be only one semitone from the tonic.

Therefore, the G must be made sharp to produce the interval of an augmented 2nd from F, and also, to make it the leading note, a semitone from A.

If we compare the scales of A major and A minor we shall see the differences.

The third note and the sixth are both one semitone lower in the minor scale than in the major.

A minor scale which starts on the same key note or tonic

as the major scale is called the *tonic minor*. When we write a tonic minor scale, we first write out the tonic major scale and then flatten (lower by one semitone) the third and sixth notes. For example:

F major

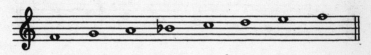

becomes F minor

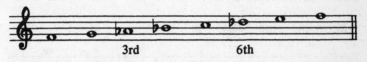

Of course, to flatten a note, we do not always use a flat. To flatten, only means to lower a note by a semitone.

D major

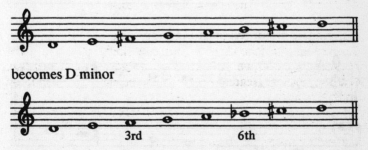

becomes D minor

Therefore, to write the harmonic minor scale of D we write as for D major except that we leave out the sharp sign before the F (flatten or lower the third) and put in a flat before the B (flatten or lower the sixth).

Each minor scale is related to a major scale and shares the same key signature. This means that the *relative minor* of any major scale is three semitones lower than the major scale. For instance, the scale of D minor (as the relative minor) shares the same key signature as F major. Similarly, E minor is the relative minor scale of G major and shares its key signature (one sharp).

Once the key signature is in place for the minor key the only note needing an accidental is the leading note, which must be raised a semitone (sharpened).

Here are the harmonic minor scales up to four sharps with their relative major keys:

A harmonic minor relative to C major

E harmonic minor relative to G major

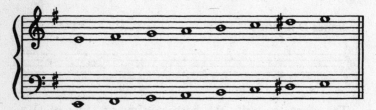

B harmonic minor relative to D major

F# harmonic minor relative to A major

C# harmonic minor relative to E major

Here are the harmonic minor scales up to four flats, with their relative major keys named:

D harmonic minor relative to F major

G harmonic minor relative to B♭ major

C harmonic minor relative to E ♭ major

F harmonic minor relative to A ♭ major

Melodic Minor Scale

This scale is different ascending (going up) from descending (coming down). Ascending, the notes follow the pattern tone, semitone, tone, tone, tone, tone, semitone.

A melodic minor – relative to C major.

To come down, the notes of the relative major are used.

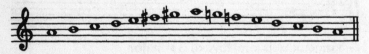

The F♯ and G♯ have to be cancelled by using the natural sign.

Another way to remember the formation of the melodic minor scale is to think of the tonic major in ascending, then one need only flatten the third. Think of the relative major descending, then one need only use the notes relevant to that scale, correcting used accidentals as necessary.

Notice that in the melodic minor scale with key signature the sixth and seventh degrees are raised a semitone ascending but lowered again in descending.

Here are the melodic minor scales up to four sharps.

A melodic minor relative to C major

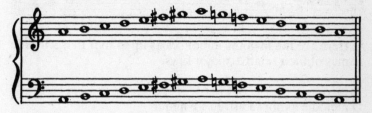

E melodic minor relative to G major

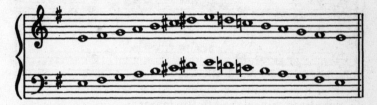

B melodic minor relative to D major

F# melodic minor relative to A major

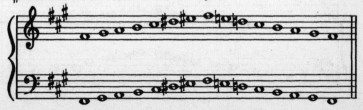

C♯ melodic minor relative to E major

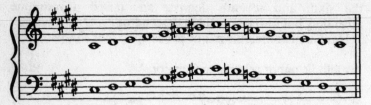

Here are the melodic minor scales up to four flats with the names of their relative major keys.

D melodic minor relative to F major

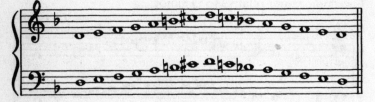

G melodic minor relative to B♭ major

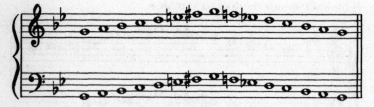

C melodic minor relative to E♭ major

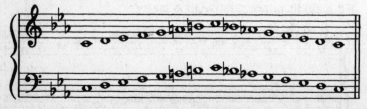

F melodic minor relative to A ♭ major

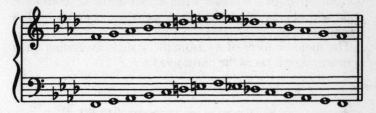

Notice that in the melodic minor scale with key signature the sixth and seventh degrees are raised a semitone ascending but lowered again in descending.

Chromatic Scale

Just as there are two forms of minor scale, so also there are two forms of chromatic scale: harmonic and melodic. The *harmonic* is so called because its semitones can be harmonised within the normal diatonic scale structure. The *melodic* was invented because it has fewer accidentals and, therefore, is easier to read. Both forms proceed entirely by semitones.

In the harmonic form we write the first degree of the scale (tonic) and fifth degree (dominant) only once; every other degree is written twice.

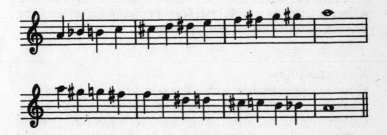

Here we have used bar lines, but no key signature. Since an accidental lasts only for the bar in which it is written, in descending, bar six needs no natural on the F.

As always in music, scale degrees are counted from the bottom upwards. We can write either form of chromatic scale with its major or minor key signature, or with no key signature.

The melodic form of a chromatic scale is ascending only: in descending it takes the harmonic form.

Notice, then, that in the melodic form the third and seventh are used only once, all other degrees twice. In descending, the harmonic form has to be used, since there is not a descending form of melodic chromatic scale.

We have learned that the major scale, the harmonic minor, melodic minor and chromatic scales are all made up of different patterns of tones and semitones. The major and both forms of minor scales are diatonic, since each note has a different letter name. Neither form of chromatic scale can be diatonic as letter names are repeated.

Recognising Keys
Music is always written with a key signature but, of course, it would be a boring composition which did not, at some point, change key (or modulate, to give the technical term), and it is this identifying of keys through which music passes that can be of great interest.

If you see two sharps at the beginning of a piece, you can assume that the key is D major or B minor. This may well change within a few bars to the key of A or B minor or another closely related key and the artistry with which this is done is a measure by which we can assess a composer's ability.

To find the key of a piece of music we look first to see if the notes fit any scale we know. For instance, we should be able to recognise the key used here by Beethoven.

Sonata opus 49 No. 2

Firstly, there is the key signature, one sharp: G major. Then the first sound is a full chord of G major, followed by notes of the second inversion of the G major tonic triad (for *Triads* see pages 64–69). However, the master does not long stay in G major; in bar eight he introduces a C♯, which, together

with the F♯ in the key signature, makes us think of the dominant key of D, though, in actual fact, the music does not actually go into D major at this point. You see how we think? An accidental added may well point the way to the music modulating (changing) to a new key. Sometimes an accidental hints at a new key but is soon cancelled by a natural or otherwise and the murmur of the key alteration is subtly led along a different path. The music does not actually change to D major after four uses and cancellations of the needed C sharp. When it does so it is not the C sharp or its cancellation which leads the way – this was just a subtle 'red herring' – but the repeated use of the dominant chord, which becomes the new tonic.

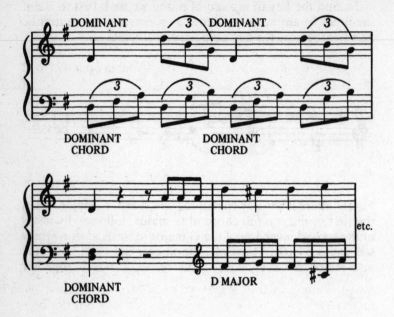

We can set out the method we use to recognise the key:

a) Key signature.
b) What do the first chords or notes show, major or minor? What do the last chords or notes show?
c) Are there any modulations (changes of key)?
d) Notice whether an accidental is part of a scale.

Decide which scale – major, melodic or harmonic minor? An accidental may mislead – it may merely be chromatic (a 'foreigner' to the key), used for effect. Notice whether the subdominant note of the original key is sharpened – this might show a change of key to the dominant.

In b) above we suggested looking at the last chord of a piece of music. This may sometimes be misleading. Nearly all music ends in the tonic key, except where a Tierce de Picardie has been used for special effect.

The Tierce de Picardie (or Picardy Third) is the tonic major chord instead of minor at the end of a composition in the minor key. This has a satisfying, final, restful effect. One must remember that it is used in minor keys and that it does not alter the key of the remainder of the music.

'Hilft mir Gott's Gute preisen' – Bach

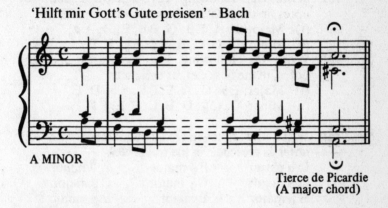

A MINOR

Tierce de Picardie
(A major chord)

Enharmonic change (giving a note or notes different names without changing the pitch) is one device used by composers when they want to change key and can use one note to pivot between the key their music is in and the new key to which they want to change.

The E♭ in bar one becomes a D♯ in bar two. Notice the use of ties and the change of key signature from E♭ major to E major, with the use of naturals to cancel the flats in the E♭ key signature. Remember to include a double bar line before the new key signature as an indication that something new is going to happen. This also applies to changes in the speed of the music between sections.

QUESTIONS

1. (a) What is a key signature?
   (b) Write the proper order of the flats in the treble, alto, tenor and bass clefs.

(c)   Write the proper order of sharps in the treble, alto, tenor and bass clefs.

2.   (a)   Write the following key signatures and key notes, in the treble clef, as minims.
    (i)   Major: F, A, E♭, G, B♭, E, D, A♭.
    (ii)   Minor: D, G, C, B, C♯, F♯, E, F.
  (b)   Write the following key signatures and key notes, in the bass clef, as crotchets.
    (i)   Major: E♭, G, A, F, B♭, A♭, D, E.
    (ii)   Minor: G, C♯, D, B, C, F, E, F♯.

3.   (a)   Write the following key signatures with key notes as crotchets in the treble clef:
    D♭ major   F♯ major   A♯ minor
    G♭ major   C♭ major   C♯ major
    E♭ major   B major   D♯ minor
    B♭ minor.
  (b)   Write the following key signatures with key notes as minims in the bass clef:
    C♯ major   G♭ major   C♭ major
    G♯ minor   B major   D♭ major
    F♯ minor   A♭ minor   E♭ minor
    A♯ minor.

4.   (a)   Name the major keys with these signatures:
    seven sharps   six flats   five sharps
    six sharps   five flats   seven flats.
  (b)   Name the minor keys with these signatures:
    seven sharps   six flats   five sharps
    six sharps   seven flats   five flats.

5.   (a)   What is a tetrachord?
  (b)   What links the two tetrachords in a major scale?

6.   (a)   What notes make up the upper tetrachord of D major?
  (b)   What notes make up the lower tetrachord of G major?
  (c)   How can we use tetrachords to produce the scale with one more sharp than G major?

7. How can we use tetrachords to produce the scale with one more flat than F major?

8. (a) Which tetrachord of which scale do we use to produce the A major scale?
   (b) How many sharps does A major have?

9. (a) Which tetrachord of which scale do we use to produce the E♭ major scale?
   (b) How many flats does E♭ major have?

10. (a) What is the order of intervals in the harmonic minor scale?
    (b) What interval must always separate the leading note from the tonic?

11. In the scale of A minor which note is the leading note?

12. (a) What is a tonic minor?
    (b) How do we write the tonic harmonic minor of a major scale?

13. (a) Which major key signature does a minor scale use?
    (b) When using the key signature to write a harmonic minor scale, which note always needs an accidental?

14. (a) What is a relative minor and how is it found?
    (b) What are the relative minor keys of the following:
    F major   E♭ major   G major
    C major   D major

15. (a) Write out the pattern used in the ascending melodic minor scale.
    (b) Which scale pattern do we use to descend?

16. In what ways do we remember the formation of the melodic minor scale?

17. What must we do to the sixth and seventh degrees of
    the melodic minor scale ascending and descending?

18. (a) What do we call the two forms of chromatic
        scale?
    (b) Why do we give each its particular name?

19. What is important to remember about the writing of
    the harmonic form of a chromatic scale?

20. What is peculiar to the melodic form of a chromatic
    scale?

21. (a) In writing the melodic chromatic scale, which
        degrees of the scale are used only once?
    (b) Is there really a descending form of melodic
        chromatic scale? If not, how do we descend?

22. Put in accidentals to make the following correctly
    written chromatic scales:

(i)

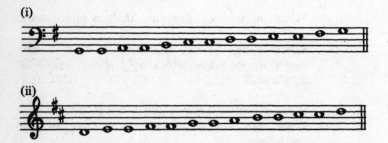

(ii)

23. Modulation is the name given to changing key during a
    piece of music. Why might we wish to change key?

24. In what keys are the following:

(i)   Beethoven Op. 40 No.1

25. What is the method we use to recognise the key of a piece of music?

26. Does music always end in the tonic key?

27. When would a Tierce de Picardie be used in music?

5

TRIADS

Formation of Triads

A triad is the basis of all harmony. A triad can be formed on any degree of the major or minor scale. They consist of the bass note, and the third and fifth notes above the bass note.

Each triad is called by the degree of the scale with which it is associated. Therefore the triad on the tonic (key note) is the tonic triad. The triad on the dominant is the dominant triad. All triads or chords can also be referred to by Roman numerals:

I = tonic triad   II = supertonic triad
III = mediant triad   IV = subdominant triad
V = dominant triad   VI = submediant triad
VII = leading note triad

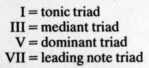

Types of Triads

It is the 3rd and 5th of a triad that designates its name and its quality. To make a major triad the interval between the root and the 3rd must be a major 3rd (four semitones), and the interval between the 3rd of the triad and the 5th, must be a minor 3rd (three semitones).

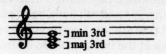

If the 3rd of the triad is flattened by one semitone, then the triad becomes minor. Thus the minor triad consists of a minor interval between the root and the 3rd, and a major interval between the 3rd and the 5th.

To make a diminished triad, two minor 3rd intervals must be used, thus making the 5th of the triad one semitone smaller as well.

An augmented triad requires two major 3rd intervals, thus making it one semitone larger than an ordinary major triad.

Major and minor triads are concordant because they are satisfactory in themselves, and need no resolution, Diminished and augmented triads are discordant or dissonant so they need a resolution chord to follow them to ensure a complete sound is made.

Position of Triads
So far all the chords have been in root position. This means

that the note from which the chord is derived is at the bottom of the triad and the 3rd and 5th have been placed above it.

However, it is possible to invert triads by placing any note other than its root at the bottom of the chord.

At example (i), the root is in the bass, therefore the triad is in root position.

At example (ii), the 3rd of the triad is in the bass, thus creating a first inversion triad.

At example (iii), the 5th of the triad is in the bass, so a second inversion triad is created.

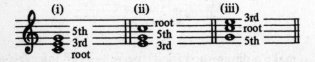

When Roman numerals are used to describe the triad, small letters are added after the number to denote the position of the triad. Root position = a, 1st inversion = b, 2nd inversion = c. In practice, however, the letter 'a' is always omitted from a root position chord, just the Roman numeral is used. In the examples below the key is G major and the chords have been identified using their Roman numerals and letters.

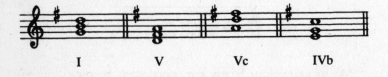

The most important triads are those whose roots are the Tonic, Dominant and Subdominant. These triads are called the primary triads.

Here are the primary triads of C major and then C minor and their inversions.

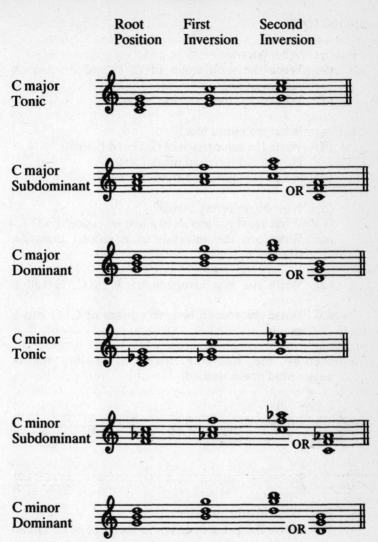

In a minor key, when using a key signature, remember always to ensure that the leading note has been raised a semitone. Here B♮ would have been needed if a key signature had been used.

QUESTIONS

1. (a) What is a triad?
    (b) Write the tonic triads of C, G and F major in root position.
    (c) What does 'root position' mean?

2. (a) What is a minor triad?
    (b) Write the tonic triads of C, G and F minor.
    (c) How are diminished triads formed?
    (d) How are augmented triads formed?

3. (a) How do we invert a triad?
    (b) What are the intervals in a first inversion triad?
    (c) What are the intervals in a second inversion triad?

4. (a) Write the first inversion triads of C, G and F major.
    (b) Write the second inversion triads of C, G and F major.

5. Identify the following triads as major, minor, augmented or diminished.

6. (a) What are the primary triads?
    (b) Write the primary triads in the keys of C, G and F major.
    (c) How do we describe the primary triads in a major key, and why?

7. Write the primary triads of G major and minor, with key signature and their inversions, and label them using Roman numerals and a letter to describe their position.

8. The following triads are in the key of G major. Identify each triad with a Roman numeral describing which degree of the scale the triad is based on, and the appropriate letter to describe the position of the triad.

6

MORE ADVANCED RHYTHMS

Triplet
Composers often want a different beat and divide it into three. One way of doing this uses a *triplet*. A triplet is a group of three notes played in the time of two of the same note value.

could become

which still has two beats in the bar but each beat has a triplet of three quavers.

Compound Time Signatures
Using the principle of the triplet

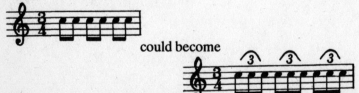

could become

The beat has now been made more complicated. So, if the composer wants to use this rhythm throughout a piece of music it is better to use a time signature which gives him beats he can divide by three. Such a beat is a dotted one.

We call such a dotted beat a *compound* beat, and the time signature using dotted beats is called a *compound* time signature.

Compound time, then, is the use of dotted beats and simple time is the use of undotted beats.

becomes

Of course, this needs a change of time signature.

The top figure of a compound time signature states how many subdivisions of the beat in each bar; it is three times that in a simple time signature. The bottom figure states the value of each subdivision. For example, $\frac{2}{4}$ becomes $\frac{6}{8}$ or three dotted crotchets.

The nine states that there are nine subdivisions of the dotted crotchet (three to each of the three crotchets). The eight states that the value of each subdivision is a quaver.

So, to find the number of beats in a bar of compound time, divide the top figure by three. To find the value of each beat divide the bottom figure by two and dot the answer.

Conversely, to find the compound equivalent time signature of a simple time signature, multiply the top figure of the simple time signature by three and the bottom figure of the simple time signature by two, thus:

$$\text{♩ ♩} \quad \frac{2}{4} \times \frac{3}{2} = \frac{6}{8} \quad \text{♩. ♩.}$$

$$\text{♩ ♩ ♩} \quad \frac{3}{4} \text{ becomes } \frac{9}{8} \quad \text{♩. ♩. ♩.}$$

$$\text{♩ ♩ ♩ ♩} \quad \frac{4}{4} \text{ becomes } \frac{12}{8} \quad \text{♩. ♩. ♩. ♩.}$$

$$\text{♪ ♪} \quad \frac{2}{8} \text{ becomes } \frac{6}{16} \quad \text{♪. ♪.}$$

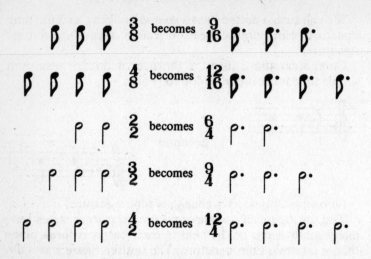

Grouping

As in simple time, grouping must show the beat. In
compound time the beat is dotted, therefore every use of the
notes and rests must show this fact.

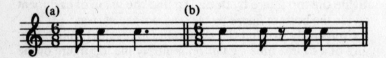

At (a) we have made a crotted dotchet beat instead of a
dotted crotchet! The quaver is the dot and must come after
the crotchet. To keep the same sound it must be written

and this plainly shows the beat.

At (b) we have really sucessfully hidden the beat, and
should have written

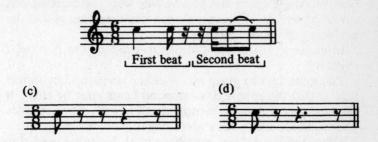

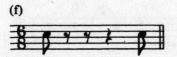

Example (c) is correct because two quaver rests were added to the quaver note to show plainly the first dotted crotchet beat. The bar was completed with a crotchet and a quaver rest; we could have used a dotted crotchet rest.

Example (d) is wrong because the beats are not properly grouped. The first beat must be completed before starting to group the rest of the bar – as in example (c).

Study the following:

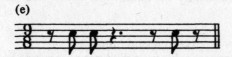

Three dotted crotchets in each bar.

(f)

Two dotted crotchets in each bar.

(g)

Four dotted crotchets in each bar.

Notice in example (f) how the bar is completed. The first beat is completed by the two quaver rests – a crotchet rest would be wrong. However, we can use a crotchet rest at the beginning of the second beat.

In example (g) notice the ties to produce the particular rhythm.

The main fact to grasp about either compound or simple time is that the simple or compound beats must be clear. If the beat can plainly be identified, all is well; if not, rewrite your values to make beats according to your time signature.

Other time signatures have been used. Holst has used $\frac{5}{4}$ in his 'Planets' Suite, Opus 32. Bartok has used $\frac{7}{8}$, $\frac{5}{8}$ and $\frac{4}{8}$ all within five bars in his 'Barcarolla' of the 'Im Freien' Suite. Constant Lambert has used $\frac{5}{8}$ in his 'Rio Grande', a choral work with solo piano in Jazz style. Any number of beats may be used in each bar so long as the beat is clear.

Like the triplet ,

notes can be grouped in many other ways. Each group has a name by which it may be identified; below are the main ones.

Duplet (only found in compound time)
A group of two notes taking up the time of three of the same kind of note.

Quadruplet (only found in compound time)
A group of four notes, either quavers or semiquavers, taking up the time of the main dotted beat.

(a)

(b)

Quintolet

In simple time, a group of five notes taking up the time of four of the same kind of note, as in example (c). In compound time, a group of five notes taking up the time of three of the same kind of note, as in example (d).

Sextolet

A group of six notes taking up the time of four of the same kind of note.

Septolet

In simple time a group of seven notes taking up the time of four of the same kind of note, as in (e). In compound time a group of seven notes taking up the time of six of the same kind of note, as in example (f).

(e)

(f)

Syncopation

We know that bar lines show the strength of the beat by being positioned immediately before each strong beat.

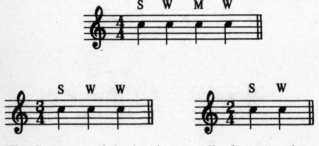

The first note of the bar is normally the strong beat. We can alter this natural order of rhythm by writing a long note where a medium or weak beat would occur:

or by the use of rests in place of the strong beat, thereby making a weak beat share the accent:

or by the use of ties, robbing the strong beat of accent

which is placed elsewhere.

We call the disturbing of the normal pattern of strong and weaker beats *syncopation*. It is a method often used in jazz and pop music today.

Our knowledge of strong beats can be used to help us put barlines into an unbarred section of music. This example has a time signature of $\frac{4}{1}$, so the two crotchets and the minim obviously fill the first bar. The next bar includes the four

quavers and minim. Bar three has the semiquavers and the three crotchets. The semibreve fills bar four. There can be no other positions for the bar lines because the semibreve must fill one bar and this fixes all the bar lines.

The minim at the end must, obviously, be at the beginning of a bar (see page 19). By working backwards we reach the crotchet at the beginning.

When we have an incomplete bar at the beginning of a piece of music we call it an *anacrusis*. Its value is added to that of the last bar to complete a full bar.

A tie can be a clue to the barring; it is often written across or through the bar line. It can only join notes of the same pitch.

When there is no time signature given, we must first notice the grouping of the notes. They will be grouped in crotchets, dotted crotchets, minims or dotted minims, or so on.

(a)

Here we can see from the dotted minim at the end that nothing else could belong to that note: certainly not the dotted crotchet which starts the notation. Also, the notes throughout are grouped as crotchets. The time signature, therefore, can be none other than $\frac{3}{4}$. The bar lines, then, come between the fourth and fifth note and thenceforth after the value of three crotchet beats.

(b)

At (b) we obviously have a compound time. The grouping of the quavers shows the beat to be a dotted crotchet. The first quaver, alone and forlorn, obviously belongs to the last crotchet, the tied one at the end. Simple arithmetic, then, shows the time signature to be $\frac{6}{8}$: the bar lines falling after the first quaver and then between the sixth and seventh note and thenceforth after the value of two dotted crotchet beats.

QUESTIONS

1. What is a triplet?

2. (a) What do we mean by a compound time signature?
   (b) What is a compound beat?

3. What is the difference between simple and compound time?

4. (a) What does the top figure of a compound time signature state?
   (b) What does the bottom figure of a compound time signature state?

5. (a) How do we find the number of beats in compound time?
   (b) How do we find the value of each beat?
   (c) Write compound time signatures which have two, three and four beats in each bar.

6. (a) How do we find the compound equivalent time signature from a simple time signature?
   (b) What are the compound time signatures relative to these simple time signatures?

   $\frac{4}{8}$; $\frac{2}{4}$; $\frac{3}{4}$; $\frac{2}{2}$; $\frac{3}{2}$; $\frac{4}{1}$.

7. Rewrite the following, correcting each to show the beat clearly:

   (i)

(ii)

(iii)

(iv)

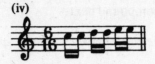

(v)

8. Correct the following:

(i)   (ii)

9. Complete the following bars:

(i)   (ii)

(iii)   (iv)

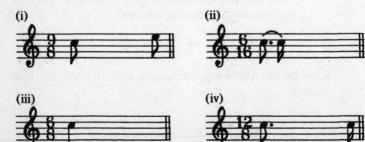

(v)   **(vi)**

10.   What must, at all times, be absolutely clear, no matter what time signature is being used?

11.   Put in time signatures:

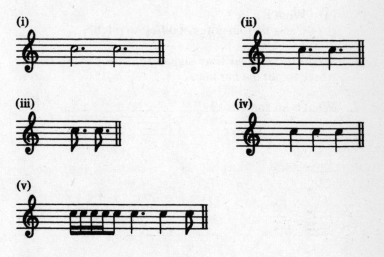

(i)   **(ii)**

(iii)   **(iv)**

(v)

(vi)

12.   (a)   What is a duplet, and in what kind of time signatures does it occur?
      (b)   What does the word quintolet mean in simple time?
      (c)   What does the word quintolet mean in compound time?
      (d)   What is a quadruplet, and in what kind of time signature does it occur?

     (e)   What is a sextolet?

     (f)   What does the word septolet mean in simple time?

     (g)   What does the word septolet mean in compound time?

13.   What would evidence of dotted beats mean as regards time signature?

14.   What does the word syncopation mean?

15.   (a)   What is a tie?

     (b)   Can a tie join notes of different pitch?

16.   When there is no time signature, how can we decide where to put the bar lines?

17.   What is an anacrusis?

7

HARMONY

Harmony is the main characteristic in music that distinguishes Western music from other types of music from all over the world. Harmony is the combination of sounds heard as chords and it looks at the relationship between the notes that make up the chords as well as the order in which they should occur. Such sounds, as in all music, must be formed to be both rhythmical and melodical.

Chords of the 7th, 9th and 13th
In addition to the normal triad that can be used in harmonic writing, it is possible to add other notes to the basic triad. One of the most important chords is that of the added 7th. This note is usually added to the dominant triad in the appropriate key.

In the key of C major, the chord of G is the dominant chord. The dominant 7th chord (V^7) is formed by the addition of the minor 7th note to the dominant chord.

V^7 in C major

This chord then becomes a dissonant chord, and must therefore be resolved. The resolution chord is normally the tonic chord.

C major V⁷   I   F major V⁷   I   G major V⁷   I

Notice how in each case the bass note rises to the tonic note, the 3rd of the first chord rises by step to the tonic note of the following chord, and the 7th note always descends by step to the 3rd of the following chord. The resolution of the 7th note of the chord is particularly important and should always be applied. It is also possible to add another 3rd to the dominant 7th chord in which case the resulting chord becomes the dominant 9th (V^9).

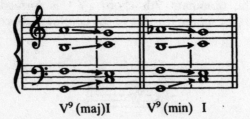

V^9 (maj)I V^9 (min) I

If another 3rd were to be added the dominant 11th (V^{11}) would be formed, and an additional 3rd would create the dominant 13th (V^{13}). These additions of thirds may be written in the major or minor key, and they resolve downwards by step like the 7th notes.

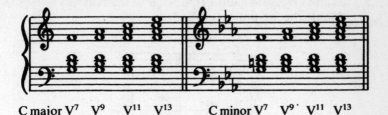

C major V⁷ V⁹ V¹¹ V¹³   C minor V⁷ V⁹ V¹¹ V¹³

Some Harmonic Rules

To sound complete, a chord derived from a triad is best written with four notes or parts. With a four-note chord, one of the voices must be doubled (used twice in the same chord) since a triad only consists of three notes.

There are some fundamental rules that need to be learnt before starting to write chords in four parts.

1. In root position chords it is advisable to double the root of the chord or the 5th, but not normally the 3rd.

2. In 1st inversion chords (the 3rd is at the bottom of the chord) double the root or the 5th, but not the 3rd.

3. In 2nd inversion chords (the 5th is at the bottom) always double the 5th but never the 3rd.

4. No two parts should proceed in 5ths or octaves. These are called consecutives and do not sound harmonically correct. However, where the same octave is repeated this is acceptable.

CONSECUTIVE 5THS   CONSECUTIVE OCTAVES   REPEATED OCTAVES

Cadences

A cadence is the completion of a phrase, sentence, or musical idea. Cadences are the musical equivalent of punctuation in speech or writing.

There are four main types of cadence: Perfect, Plagal, Imperfect and Interrupted.

1. Perfect Cadence (full close) uses chords V–I, or V⁷–I, and is the most complete sounding of all the cadences.

V   I   V⁷   I

2. Plagal Cadence uses chords IV–I, and is often found at the end of hymns.

IV   I   IV   I

3. Imperfect Cadence (half close) uses chords I–V or IV–V.

I   V   IV   V

4. Interrupted Cadence uses chords V–VI. It sounds initially as if a Perfect Cadence is going to be played with the use of the dominant chord, but then the music completely changes direction with the use of the submediant chord (VI).

V   VI   V   VI

There is one other cadence that can be used. It is called the Phrygian Cadence, and is only found in the minor key. It uses the chords IVb–V, and is really an Imperfect Cadence in the minor key.

IVb   V

The penultimate chord in any cadential progression is on a weak beat of the bar, with the final chord being on a strong beat. The only exception to this is when a *feminine ending* is used. It can be applied to any cadence, the difference being that the final chord ends on the weak beat of the bar.

More Ways of Writing Chords
It is possible to write chords in a broken or arpeggiated form as well as all the notes sounding together at the same time. Here are some examples. An arpeggiated version of a chord is when the notes of a triad are used in an ascending or descending order.

Broken chords can occur in a number of ways.

One type of broken chord writing became very popular in keyboard music of the 18th Century. Indeed, it was named after the Italian composer who invented it, Domenico Alberti. The style is called an Alberti bass. On the piano it occurs in the lefthand, and uses notes of the triad in a repetitive format.

Chromatic Chords

A chromatic chord can be made up from a diatonic chord by adding one or more accidentals but without changing the key. Thus in C major, chord II can be made into a chromatic chord by making the minor chord into a major one with the introduction of the F♯.

    II   II made major

When, as in the example above, the addition of a chromatic note makes the chord major, it often becomes the dominant chord in a V–I progression. When this occurs, these chords that function as a dominant are known as secondary dominants. They do not necessarily create a feeling of modulation, they simply add colour to the chordal progressions. They can occur on chords II, III, VI and also Ib.

  I II V I   I II V I
                         (maj)

The Neopolitan 6th Chord

This is the 1st inversion of a major chord on the flattened supertonic (♭ IIb).

Although it can be used in both major and minor keys it is more common for it to be used in minor ones. It is often found closely related to cadential progressions, for example:

    ♭ IIb–Ic–V–I in C major.

    I– ♭IIb–V–I in C minor.

♭IIb   Ic   V   I   I ♭IIb V   I

The Augmented 6th Chord

There are three versions of the augmented 6th chord. They mostly occur on the minor 6th degree of the scale. Since it is an augmented chord, it must resolve. Normally the two notes forming the augmented 6th interval resolve outwards to form an octave.

Italian 6th consists of: major 3rd and augmented 6th above the bass note.

ITALIAN 6TH It. 6th V V^7 I

French 6th consists of: major 3rd, augmented 4th and augmented 6th above the bass note.

FRENCH 6TH Fr. 6th V V^7 I

German 6th consists of: major 3rd, perfect 5th and
                         augmented 6th above the bass
                         note.

The German 6th chord is always the first chord of three,
making an approach chord to a Perfect or Interrupted
Cadence.

GERMAN 6TH Ger. 6th Ic V^7 I

The Diminished 7th Chord

The diminished 7th chord is made up of three minor 3rds on
top of each other.

The chord is dissonant and must therefore be resolved, since
it contains not only the interval of a diminished 7th

but also two diminished 5ths

It is normal for the diminished 7th interval to resolve inwards to form a perfect 5th, and for the two diminished 5th intervals also to resolve inwards to form major or minor 3rds.

Other Forms of Notation

The Roman numeral symbols that have been used so far are never used in performance. Instead there are two ways of notating music in shorthand. One derives from Jazz and 'Popular' music, the other derives from a period in music known as the Baroque (17th century – middle of the 18th century), and is called Figured Bass or Thorough Bass.

The aim of both these types of notation is to give the performer information regarding the chords that should be used whilst allowing free improvisation or decoration in the melody line or in the chords.

Jazz Notation

The chords used in Jazz music are usually fairly simple. More complex chord structures are obtained by improvisation on what is already given in the music.

The letter name of the chord is shown as a capital letter. The chord is then assumed to be major unless a small 'm' is placed after the letter name, making the chord minor. If a '+' or 'aug' is used after the letter name, then the chord is augmented, and if an 'o' or 'dim' is used then the chord is diminished.

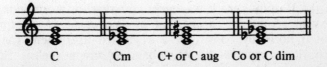

C   Cm   C+ or C aug   Co or C dim

Sometimes notes are added in addition to the basic chord desired by a composer. These additions are shown by a number next to the letter name, C^6. This means that a chord of a C major should be played (C, E, G) plus the sixth note from C which is A.

C⁶

When the figure 7 is used in conjunction with a letter, G^7, it refers to the minor 7th from the letter name (G, B, D, F). If the major 7th interval from the letter name was required it would be written as $Gmaj^7$ (G, B, D, F $\sharp$).

G⁷   maj⁷

Sometimes a composer will want to specify which bass note to use. This is achieved by writing the chord description as normal, then placing the letter name of the specific bass note after an oblique stroke (/), Cm/G (a C minor chord is required with a G in the bass).

Cm/G

Figured Bass

In the Baroque era it was most common for a continuo to play in all music, except that of solo music. A continuo would normally consist of a keyboard instrument (harpsichord or organ) and a string bass instrument (cello). Both players would be given a single line of music in the bass clef. The keyboard player would be required to 'realise' the bass line by playing the given part in the left hand and by adding chords above, whilst the string player would just play the bass line.

The keyboard player could determine which chords the composer desired from the bass line because underneath each note figures were written. These figures represented the intervals the additional notes had to be above the bass notes.

Root Position Chord

This means that the chord above the bass note consists of a C, the 3rd (E) and the 5th (G). Since this style of writing is a form of shorthand a root position chord is also recognised either by the figures $\frac{5}{3}$ or by having no figures underneath the note concerned. The extra notes can be played in a number of ways.

1st Inversion Chord

This means that the chord above the bass consists of the 3rd (G) and the 6th (C). It is important to remember that the E in the bass must not be doubled since it is the 3rd of the basic chord of C in root position. The C should be doubled and the chord formed may look like these:

The $\frac{6}{3}$ chord is often notated as a 6 on its own underneath the appropriate bass note.

2nd Inversion Chord

This means that the chord above the bass note consists of the 4th (C) and the 6th (E). The bass note must be doubled. When harmonising passages of music this chord should be used sparingly, and is only generally found at cadence points.

Chords of the 7th

These chords have their own figures since they use an additional note (the 7th) to the basic chords just discussed, and this note must be notated in the figuring that occurs below the bass note.

Root Position Chord of the 7th

This means that the 3rd (B), the 5th (D) and the 7th (F) are played above the bass note. It is more common for this chord to be figured simply as 7.

1st Inversion Chord of the 7th

This means that the 3rd (D), the 5th (F) and the 6th (G) above the bass note will be played. This chord is normally notated as $\frac{6}{5}$.

2nd Inversion Chord of the 7th

This means that the 3rd (F), the 4th (G) and the 6th (B) will be played above the bass note. This chord is normally figured $\frac{6}{4}$.
$_3$

3rd Inversion Chord of the 7th

This means that the 2nd (G), the 4th (B) and the 6th (D) will be played above the bass note. This chord is normally figured as $\begin{smallmatrix}6\\4\\2\end{smallmatrix}$.

Notating Accidentals

To write in an accidental using figures, the appropriate accidental is normally written to the left of the figure it concerns, but it can also come after the figure. If an accidental is written directly under the bass note it refers to the 3rd note above the bass note.

In 1st inversion chords where the normal figuring is a 6, a chromatically altered 3rd is notated by writing the accidental underneath the 6.

A stroke through the figure (/) means that the note should be raised by one semitone.

A diminished 7th chord is written as 7̸ to avoid confusion with the root position 7th chord.

As a general rule, to find the root of a fully figured triad, find the lowest even number in the figure:

in root position 8 is the root
in 1st inversion 6 is the root
in 2nd inversion 4 is the root

Suspensions

A suspension occurs when one note of a chord is delayed from moving whilst the other notes change to a new chord and create a dissonance due to the tied note.

Below are two progressions each using the same chords. However, in the second progression the G is tied over to the next chord, suspended before it resolves down to the F$\sharp$.

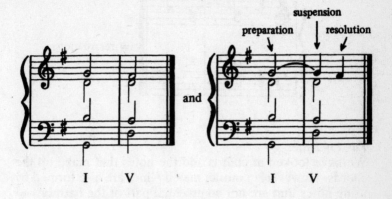

There are three notes involved in creating suspensions:

1. the preparation note which must always be part of the chord
2. the suspension which is the same note tied over
3. the resolution note which is always part of the new chord.

The resolution note is always reached by a step either downwards (a true suspension) or upwards (known as a retardation). The examples below show how the chords would be notated using figures. Remember that the figures show the intervals from the bass note.

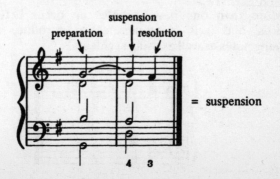

= suspension

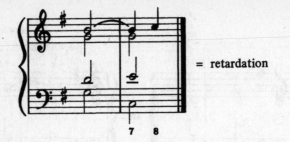

= retardation

Passing Notes

We have looked at chords and the notes that make up the chords. However, in music, melody lines are also formed by using notes that are not an essential part of the harmony of the chords underneath, and therefore add a little dissonance to the music. These notes are known as passing notes. They can occur in the melody line as well as the bass line.

The simplest type of passing note is one that links two harmony notes that are a third apart.

More than one passing note can occur between two chords, and it is quite possible to introduce chromatic passing notes as well as using accidentals.

The Sequence

A sequence is the immediate repetition of a pattern of notes either at a higher or lower interval. It can occur in the melody line (melodic sequence) or in the chords (harmonic sequence), and can also be combined in both.

This device was particularly common in the Baroque era when composers used it to help them modulate (change key) in the music.

The most popular type of sequence is when a root position chord is used and is then followed by a chord a 4th higher or 5th lower. The brackets (⌐_____⌐) show the secondary dominants that occur in this type of progression (V–I), and these can be used in conjunction with changing key.

Modulation

A modulation refers to a change of key in the music. For a modulation to occur it is necessary to introduce the sharpened leading note (7th note) of the new key, and to complete the modulation with a perfect cadence in the new key.

In each of the examples below the first chord is the 'pivot chord'. This term is applied to the chord that can be related to both keys, the old key and the new key, thus it acts as a pivot between the two keys.

Key = C major, modulates to A minor

In C major   I
In A minor III   V⁷   I

Key = C major, modulates to G major

In C major   I
In G major IV   V⁷   I

Key = C major, modulates to E minor

In C major   I
In E minor VI   IV   V⁷   I

Key = C major, modulates to F major

In C major   I
In F major   V   V⁷   I

Key = C major, modulates to D minor

In C major   I
In D minor VII   V⁷   I

Before modulating it is necessary to decide on the new key. Every key has two closely related keys, the dominant and the subdominant. These keys, combined with their relative minor keys, make up the five related keys.

Thus, in C major, the related keys are:

F major (subdominant)   G major (dominant)
D minor (relative to F major)
E minor (relative to G major)
and A minor (relative minor of C major)

Similarly, from C minor:

F minor (subdominant)   G minor (dominant)
A ♭ major (relative major of F minor)
B ♭ major (relative major of G minor)
and E ♭ major (relative major of C minor)

QUESTIONS

1. Write out the dominant 7th, 9th, 11th and 13th chords in the keys of D major and D minor.

2. Which notes do we usually double, in each case, when writing root position, first inversion and second inversion chords?

3. Which two types of intervals should you avoid using consecutively?

4. Which chords form the following?
    (i)   perfect cadence
    (ii) imperfect cadence
    (iii) plagal cadence
    (iv) interrupted cadence.

5. What is a phrygian cadence?

6. When is a feminine ending used?

7. Name two ways of writing chords which vary from the normal triadic form.

8. How are secondary dominants formed?

9. What does ♭ IIb stand for?

10. There are three augmented 6th chords. Name them and state the differences between them.

11. Which intervals are used to form the diminished 7th chord?

12. On the stave below write the correct symbols that would identify these chords for a Jazz musician.

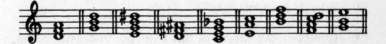

13. Figure the following chords correctly using figured bass.

14.   Write in the chords that correspond to these figures.

15.   What names are given to the three notes that are used to form suspensions?

16.   What is the name given to a suspension that resolves upwards?

17.   What is a passing note?

18.   Complete the chords of this sequence and write in the chord symbols.

19.   Write down the five related keys of the following:
       (i)   F major
       (ii)   E minor.

8

VOCAL AND
PART WRITING

Vocal Ranges

The human voice can be divided into four main categories:

    Soprano – high, female (a boy sings treble);

    Contralto/Alto – low, female;

    Tenor – high, male;

    Bass – low, male.

These, and two additional ranges, are approximately the following.

In a choir or any ensemble of voices (or instruments) each is called a part. In vocal writing the bass and soprano are the outside and the tenor and contralto the inside parts.

Below are four bars of four-part vocal writing in close, or piano, score. Notice the curved bracket { joining both staves together implying that if played on a keyboard instrument both staves should be played.

BAXTER

Below shows how the music would appear in open, or vocal, score. The tenor part uses the treble clef but with an eight underneath it. This is because the tenor part is written an octave higher than it is sung. Notice that only the straight bracket is used since all four parts are sung by different voices.

BAXTER

When writing music for four parts but using the close, or piano, score the stems of the soprano and tenor notes should be turned up, but the stems of the contralto and bass should be turned down. Unison (parts sounding the same note) may need two stems, but if the note is a semibreve write two notes, one for each part.

When writing four parts in open, or vocal score, the stems of the notes should be turned up or down according to their position on the stave. Below the middle line – stem upwards: above the middle line – stem downwards. On the middle line – either up or down, according to the pattern on either side.

Sometimes, one may be asked to write in open score for string quartet. In this case, the parts are: bass, treble or tenor clefs for violoncello; alto clef for viola; treble clefs for the second and first violins.

BAXTER

Overlapping
This occurs when a part horizontally goes below or above the part next to it, like, for instance:

Here, the Soprano (Treble) starts on the dominant and then immediately falls below the tonic, which was heard from the Contralto (Alto) part in the previous chord.

Crossing of Parts
This occurs when a part is higher than the voice it would normally be beneath, or lower than the voice it would normally be above, like, for instance:

Crossing can occur between any parts other than between the two outer ones, but is usually between vertically adjacent parts.

Such treatment has many times been used by composers for special technical reasons, but as a general harmonic rule overlapping and crossing of parts should be avoided because to do so blurs the melodic line of the parts concerned.

QUESTIONS

1. Name the four ranges of the human voice, and describe each.

2. Give the approximate ranges of the following voices:
Soprano   Tenor   Contralto
Baritone   Mezzo Soprano   Bass

3. (a) What name do we give to the notes to be played by a particular member of an ensemble (choir, quartet, etc.)?
   (b) In what vertical order are the notes for each type of voice printed when written for a four part choir? Start with the lowest sounding voice.

4. In what type of score is the following written?

5. (a) Write the previous example on open, or vocal, score.
   (b) Which clef do the alto and tenor singers use today?

6. (a) Using a piano score, how should the stems of notes in the soprano and tenor parts be written?
   (b) Using a piano score, how should the stems of notes in the alto and bass parts be written?
   (c) How should unison notes be shown in a piano score?

7. (a) How should stems be written on notes in open score?

   (b) What is the difference between the words unison and octave?

8. String quartets are always written in open score. Which clefs are used for each instrument – Violoncello, Viola, First and Second Violins?

9. (a) What is meant by overlapping?

   (b) Give an example of overlapping with explanation.

10. (a) What is meant by crossing of parts?

    (b) Give an example of crossing of parts with explanation.

11. What detrimental effect can be brought about by allowing parts to overlap?

9

TRANSPOSITION

This may be explained as the rewriting of a composition, or part of a composition, at a pitch different from the original.

Transposition between Clefs

Here is an exercise which would be easier to read if it were written in the treble clef because of all the leger lines. Firstly, we write the treble clef, then fix the pitch of the first note, which here happens to be middle C. The rest is only a matter of being careful to transcribe each note carefully on to its rightful place on the treble stave.

In our examples we had no accidentals, but these need cause us no trouble if we are careful to identify the note concerned and think about its pitch. The commonest error in transposing from one clef to another is in transcribing to the correct pitch. For example, (a) is the F above middle C, not the F below middle C as shown at (b) and at (c) the A is that two A's below middle C, not as shown at (d) which is only one A below middle C.

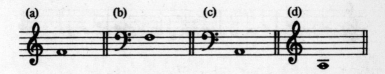

So remember to be careful in fixing the pitch of each note you write. Consider how far above or below middle C is the note being transcribed. Take into consideration the alteration made by use of the new clef. Read most carefully what you are asked to do. Be careful not to rewrite an octave higher when you are really asked to rewrite at the pitch of one octave lower.

We may want to write the following passage in the treble clef to sound an octave higher.

The first note is a C. One octave higher is middle C. The passage then rises up the major scale by tone, tone, semitone, tone to G, which note is repeated. The next note is one tone higher, A, and falls by tone, tone to F. It then rises a major 3rd back to A and falls back to G. The next passage consists of a tone down, a minor 3rd down, a tone up, a major 3rd down, a tone up, a tone down, a tone up, a minor 3rd down, a semitone up.

Thus we transpose by interval.

Similarly, (a) written an octave lower becomes (b).

(a)

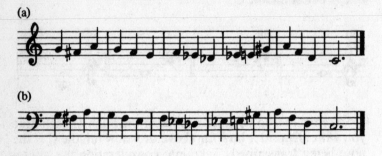

(b)

Firstly, in order to transpose, one must determine the key of the original, see page 56.

The following example is in G major. We can see this by the key signature: there is one sharp – F♯, and the last note is G. We can now decide the key of the transposition we intend.

Let us transpose up a semitone: this means our new key is to be A♭ major (there is no key of G♯ major). Looking at the original, we find the first note is the mediant of G major, so our first note – after putting in our new key signature of four flats – must also be the mediant which, in the key of A♭, is the note C.

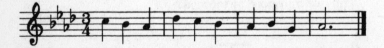

Having determined our first note, we may proceed by interval for each new note. The second note in G major is one tone below the first note. For our second note in the transposition, we must also descend one tone, which, in our new key, is B♭.

When we are finished, we should check our work by going over each note as we did the first. Original is mediant, have we transposed by using the mediant of the new key? Second note is supertonic, have we transposed by using the new supertonic? Third note is tonic, have we used tonic of new key? And so on.

If accidentals have been used, the effect of the accidental in the original must be reproduced in the transposition.

The above example is in the key of D minor. We will transpose down a semitone, which means our new key will be C♯ minor.

In the original the first note was a minor 3rd above the tonic, so in our transposition – after putting in the new key signature – the first note must also be a minor 3rd above the tonic, which in C♯ minor is the note E. We can then proceed to complete the rest of the transposition by interval for each new note. In the original the second note is a minor 3rd below the first note – the tonic, in fact. So the second note of our transposition must also be the tonic, which in C♯ minor is C♯.

The transposition can continue by interval but it is advisable to make very sure of the transposition of accidentals by checking that the interval moved has been correctly transcribed and also that they are the same interval from the new tonic as is the note in the original version from the original tonic.

Our first accidental here is B♮ in the third bar. This, in the original version, is a tone above the previous note so in the transposed version a tone up from G♯ must be used – A♯. As a further check, notice that the B♮ of the original is a major 6th above the tonic; so the transposition to A♯ is correct – it is a major 6th above our new tonic.

Likewise, with the C♯: it is one semitone below the previous note and is the leading note of the old key. Our transposition must be one semitone below C♯ and be the leading note: B♯ is correct. Finally, the E♭: it is a diminished 3rd above the previous note and the flattened supertonic of the old key. In the transposition, therefore, the correct note must be a diminished 3rd above the previous note and be the flattened supertonic of our new key. D♮ is correct.

A double sharp or double flat need cause no consternation but may be transposed in exactly the way taught here: first by interval from the previous note and then checked by its interval from the tonic.

transposed down a tone:

The double flat is one semitone below the previous note, it is also a flattened dominant, so the transposition must be the same.

Remember that when key signatures are used, an accidental will occur in the transposed version only where one appears in the original.

Transposing Instruments

Before leaving transposition, it should be known that there are instruments for which the music is normally written in a key or octave other than that at which they sound. These are called transposing instruments and include many wind instruments not pitched in C – such as clarinets in B♭, E♭ and A, horns in F, trumpets in B♭ and D, piccolo (which sounds an octave higher than the written notation), as well as double bass (which sounds an octave lower than the written notation).

The need for transposing instruments originated in early musical times when only natural notes were available to players of certain wind instruments. Today these instruments have valves and keys which ensure better tuning and provide a greater range than the earlier models. The basic principle is that the written note C actually sounds the note named in the description of the instrument. A trumpet in B♭, playing a written C, sounds B♭ (a tone lower than is written). A horn in F, playing a written C, sounds F (a 5th lower than written). Music for the double bass is written an octave higher than it sounds to avoid using many leger lines – the bottom note of the double bass sounds

   and is written

Clarinet in B♭	sounds one tone lower than written.
" in A	sounds minor 3rd " " "
" in E♭	sounds minor 3rd higher " "
Trumpet in B♭	sounds one tone lower " "
" in D	sounds one tone higher " "
" in C	is *not* transposing
Horn in F	sounds perfect 5th lower than written.
Piccolo	sounds one octave higher than written.
Double Bass	sounds one octave lower than written.

QUESTIONS

1. What is transposition?

2. Before we can transpose a piece of music to another pitch, what fact must we know?

3. In what key are the following?

(i)

(ii)

(iii)

4. After having determined the first note of a transposition how should we proceed?

5. How can we check the accuracy of our transpositions?

6. Must the interval from tonic to a note with an accidental be the same in a transposed version?

7. (a)   Rewrite the following melody an octave lower, using the bass clef:

(b) Rewrite the following melody an octave higher,
      using the treble clef:

8. (a) Rewrite this an octave higher, still using the
        treble clef:

(b) Rewrite this an octave lower, still using the bass
      clef:

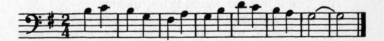

9. Rewrite the following at a pitch one semitone higher.
    Use the new key signature and explain how each note is
    transposed.

10. (a) What is the key of the following?

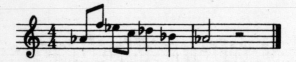

(b) What would the new key be if it were transposed up a minor 3rd?

11. (a) How do we check the transposition of accidentals?
(b) Are any accidentals necessary in a transposed version of the example in question 10(a), when the key signature is used?

12. How do we transpose a double sharp or a double flat?

13. With a key signature, when will an accidental appear in the transposed version of a piece?

14. (a) What is meant by the description 'transposing instrument'?
(b) Name three transposing instruments.
(c) How is music for double bass written and why?
(d) Using a bass stave, write the lowest note sounded by the double bass, and then the note as it would be written.
(e) Write out this as it would sound played by a Clarinet in B♭.

10

RHYTHMS WITH WORDS

A lot of music is sung, and as this uses words, we must now learn to write rhythms to fit words.

> 'In the sea I caught a flea,
> What a funny place for it to be.'

We must first read the words aloud several times so that the natural rhythm is found. Certain words will be more accented than others. One way of saying it would be:

> '*In* the sea I | *caught* a flea; |
> *What* a funny place for | *it* to be.' | |

We know that a strong beat (or accent) always follows a bar line so we can put in the bar lines above.

In bar one we have four words which are equal – perhaps four crotchets would fit this. Then bar two must be two crotchets and a minim. Bar three has four fast and two slow sounds so four quavers and two crotchets will fill the bar. Bar four is two crotchets and a minim. The time signature is obviously $\frac{4}{4}$.

In   the   sea   I   caught   a   flea,

What   a   fun - ny   place   for   it   to   be.

Here, nearly every word has one note; 'funny', however, needs two because there are two sounds or syllables in the word. We must be careful to give one note to every syllable of every word.

This example has words with several syllables.

'I like walking, it makes me very fit.'

The word 'walking' has two syllables, so has 'very'. It is not the length of a word but the separate sounds we make when we say the word which are the syllables.

Say the sentence above several times and the accents may fall as here:

I   like   wal - king __, it   makes me ve - ry   fit.

Notice the syncopation in bar two and the way we write the words, separating the syllables with a hyphen.

Word setting is easy if certain rules are followed. Follow these:

(a) Read the words many times until a particular rhythmic way of saying them is fixed in your mind.

(b) Mark the accented words or syllables.

(c) Put a bar line before each strong accent.

(d) Write a suitable time signature and start writing the rhythm, making certain that each bar is complete and correctly grouped.

(e) Quavers and shorter values should be separated when each note is a different word or syllable.

QUESTIONS

1. Put these words to the tunes below. Write each syllable exactly under the note to which it refers:

(i)
'Bobby Shaftoe's gone to sea'

(ii)
'Oh dear, what can the matter be? Johnny's so long at the fair'

(iii)
'Lucy Locket lost her pocket, Kitty Fisher found it'

(iv)
'All the birds of the air were a sighing and a sobbing, when they heard of the death of poor Cock Robin.'

2. Write note values to the following words. Be careful to put the words, or syllables, exactly under the notes to which you intend them to belong:

   (i) 'Mary had a little lamb, she thought it was a goat; it ended up as mutton chops and a sheepskin coat.'

   (ii) 'Ant and Rabbit, Lamb and Mouse, Horse and Kangaroo; Chimpanzee and Ape and Rat – all are in the zoo.'

3. (a) How should quavers and shorter note values be written when making the rhythm of words?

   (b) Which of these note patterns (i or ii) best fits the words below? Say why.

(i)

Some people like the sound of bells, some people cannot bear them.

(ii)

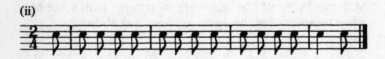

11

PHRASING

As with all the Arts, successful music consists of its various features balanced and contrasted to form a whole. This balance exists both within the complete piece and also within each component part, and it is necessary here to study the balance created within melodies, for these make up the main structure of any music.

If we examine a well known tune, such as the opening of the Andante of Haydn's 'Surprise' Symphony, we can see the balance between the two halves of the main tune, which are described as A and B.

There is a very similar rhythm in both halves, there is an identical opening to each half, and it is only in the second half that any alteration is made.

If we wish to add a balanced and suitable continuation to a melody, a practice usually called 'adding an answering phrase', we must observe the following procedure. First, commence our continuation by using the opening of the given melody. For example – if the given melody is:

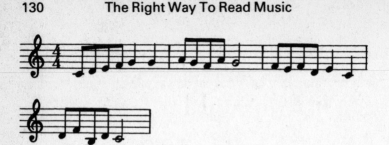

we can continue:

The next stage is to introduce a modulation, usually to the dominant (in this case G major) if the tonic key is major. By incorporating some rhythmic features of the original our addition becomes the same in length as the given portion.

Thus the complete tune is:

We can see, therefore, that any music we add must balance the given portion both in rhythm and length.

To be a little more musical we can use, at the beginning of our continuation, only the rhythm of the opening. Here the given opening is:

We can add:

The melody given may, of course, modulate to a related key (often to the dominant or relative major/minor). If it does this we may be asked to write a suitable ending to the given melody. In this case we must add music which will return us to the original key.

The following tune, in A minor, modulates to C major at the eighth bar.

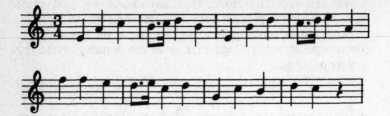

This can be identified in three ways:

bar 7 – a G is used. If the music was still in A minor its leading note (G) would have been sharpened.

bar 8 – the penultimate note is a D. This belongs to the chord of G major which is the dominant chord of C major.

– Since this melody modulates to C major it is necessary to have a perfect cadence in the new key (V–I). Thus a G major chord is followed by a C major chord.

If we are to write a suitable ending to this opening we must add another eight bars, modulating back to A minor. Remember that, in order to modulate from one key to another, we must use a note foreign to the first key but fitting into the new key. In the example below, this note will be a G sharp, the leading note of A minor.

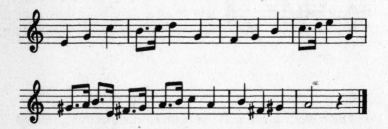

In this ending we have added music which balances the opening in rhythm and length but also contrasts with it, using the dotted quaver/semiquaver pattern.

We may be asked to add an ending to a melody which does not actually modulate in the given part. If we have sufficient length, eight bars or more, we should try to introduce, at least, the idea of a different key even if we do not actually modulate to it, before concluding the melody.

Here we have used a fleeting reference to D minor (using a C$\sharp$) to produce a more interesting ending.

At bars 13 and 14 there is a device known as melodic sequence. The melody of bar 13 is repeated in bar 14 a tone lower. Sequences can be as short as one bar or as long as a complete phrase or sentence, the essential point being the repeat of a melodic pattern at a different pitch. If the melody is not quite the same in outline, but the rhythm is identical, we use the term rhythmic sequence.

We also use the term 'sequence' to refer to a progression of chords, repeated at a different pitch. This is called a harmonic sequence.

QUESTIONS

1. (a) What two features are essential in any success-
       ful Art form?
   (b) What makes up the main structure of music?

2. Copy these tunes and mark off with A and B the phrase
   of each tune:

(i)

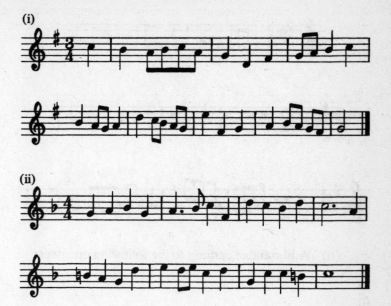

(ii)

3. (a) What term do we use to describe the addition of a balanced and suitable continuation to a melody?
    (b) In what way can we use the given opening to help us with our continuation?
    (c) How can we introduce some interest into our continuation?
    (d) What must we remember when we continue a melody?

4. In what way can we be more musical than merely to copy out the opening of the melody?

5. (a) If the given portion modulates to a related key and we are to add an ending, what must our melody do before concluding?
    (b) In order to modulate clearly what must we do?

6. (a) Add answering phrases to these openings:

(b)   Add suitable endings to the following openings:

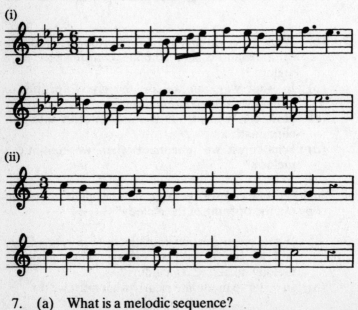

7.   (a)   What is a melodic sequence?
     (b)   What is a rhythmic sequence?

(c) What is a harmonic sequence?
(d) Under the following melody mark all the
     sequences and identify their type as either
     melodic or rhythmic.

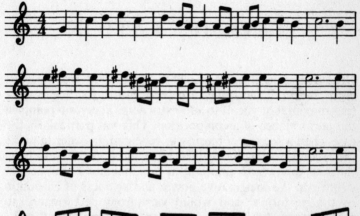

12

ORNAMENTATION

Ornamentation in music is used to decorate musical ideas. In early music it was the accepted norm for the soloist (instrumental or vocal) to add extra notes at certain points in the performance of a composition. This was particularly the case when a section of music was repeated, in order to make the second hearing more decorative and thus different from the first time. Such impromptu ornamentation was dependent upon the imaginative power and ableness of execution of the performer and would vary from performance to performance. Early composers were, to some extent, satisfied to leave this decorating of their music to competent performers, but gradually signs were evolved to represent in writing as near as possible every kind of acceptable embellishment.

Some modern composers write out in full exactly what they intend to be played. Others, however, use the standardised signs discussed below.

The Appoggiatura
This ornament is written as a tiny note, ♪, of the value it is to sound. Unlike the similar looking acciaccatura (see opposite) it is part of the melody. Thinking of the note before which the appoggiatura is placed as the principal note, the appoggiatura takes half the value of a principal note which is divisible by two.

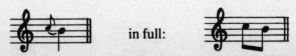

in full:

If the principal note is dotted, the appoggiatura takes two thirds the value.

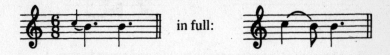 in full:

Should the principal note be tied, the appoggiatura takes the value of the longer of the tied notes.

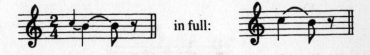 in full:

When the appoggiatura is written with a chord, it takes the place of the note to which it is joined by a slur.

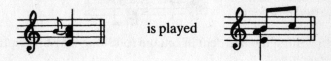 is played

The Acciaccatura

This is an ornament written as a tiny note like the appoggiatura but with a stroke through its stem. The musical intention may be understood by knowing that acciaccatura comes from the word *acciaccare* – to crush. In performance one crushes in the ornament as much as possible on the beat. There is, however, bound to be a certain anticipation and this is not undesirable if it is minute and the result is a crisp accenting of the principal note.

If you must show the acciaccatura in full, for examination purposes, for example, it is customary to show it as detracting from the principal note by one demisemiquaver.

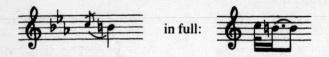   in full:

The Mordent (Upper mordent ⬥) (Lower mordent ⬥)
Three notes played in the time of the principal note.

(i)   the principal note
(ii)   the note above (for an upper mordent) or the note
       below (for a lower mordent);
(iii) the principal note.

                                                    in full:

Upper mordent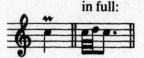

                                          in full:

Lower mordent
(also known as an
inverted mordent)

   In writing the mordent in full the following may be helpful
to remember.
   Tempo slower than Allegro (see page 174): halve and dot
the principal note. Give the remaining value to the first two
notes of the ornament – (a).
   Tempo Allegro or quicker: halve the principal note value
and give the remaining value to the first two notes of the
ornament – (b).

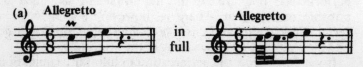

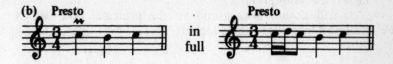

A double mordent – 〰〰 or 〰〰 – merely repeats the first mordent. The note values normally follow the rule: halve the principal note and give the remaining value to the first four notes of the ornament.

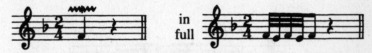

The upper or lower note (in an upper or lower mordent respectively) is always diatonic to the key and is determined by the key signature.

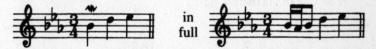

To alter the upper or lower note (as necessary) we add the appropriate accidental above (or below) the sign for the ornament.

The Trill (or Shake)

An ornament of two notes, principal note and the note above. These are played quickly, one after the other, and are indicated by the first two letters of the word written over the principal note.

The amount of alterations put into a trill depends upon the value of the principal note and the tempo of the music. For tempo less than allegro, use demisemiquavers. For allegro or faster, use semiquavers.

A trill should always end on the principal note unless followed by a note a third higher.

In this case, omit the last repetition of the principal note.

In the music of Mozart's time the trill was begun on the note above the principal note.

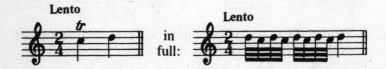

This produces an even number of notes, ending on the principal note.

In later music the trill is intended to begin on the principal note. This results in an uneven number of notes in the last group and, therefore, the writing of a triplet.

To make a musical rendering, the triplet falls on the first, second and third of the last five notes.

In full:

Of course, if the principal note is immediately preceded by a note of the same pitch it would not be musical to begin a trill on that note, but on the note above, as in earlier times.

If the trill is immediately preceded by an acciaccatura, that note must be considered to be the first note of the trill.

If the principal note is prolonged, either by a dot or a tie, the trill should continue for the total value.

If a composer wants a trill to end with a turn (see page 144), he will write the principal note either with its full value and indicate the turn by two tiny notes which may be of any value, but usually a semiquaver or demisemiquaver; or he will show the last two notes as normal sized notes and detract their value from the principal note.

In full:

If a turn is added at the end of a trill, the notes are of the same value and are grouped in the same way as in the basic trill.

Unless a turn is indicated in either way above, no turn should be introduced.

Normally a trill, with or without a turn added at the end,

uses notes diatonic to the key of the music.

Sometimes, however, to change key (modulate) a composer alters the upper note of the trill by placing an accidental above the sign.

Notice that, in the example above, the trill starts on the upper note (the normal practice) and, because of the speed, uses semiquavers and is only four notes – sounding like a four note turn (see below). This example has enabled the composer to modulate from D major to C major.

The Turn

The notes of a turn depend much on the tempo of the music in order to determine their value. There are many variations of the turn not only in how it is played, but also when it is played. The basic sign for the turn is ∾, however it can also be inverted, turned upside-down, ⌀, and include accidentals. A turn can also be placed directly over a note or between two notes. Here are the variations the basic turn sign can have:

(a) ∾   (b) ∾   (c) ∾   (d) ∾

(e) ∾   (f) ∾   (g) ∾   (h) ∾

(i) ∾   (j) ∾   (k) ∾

plus the sharps, flats and natural signs with the sign ⌀ and each of these can be written over a note or between notes:

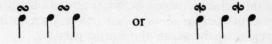

The Turn written over a note

If a turn is written over a note, it is both written and played as a group of four notes in the following order:

(i)   the note above the principal note;
(ii) the principal note;
(iii) the note below;
(iv) the principal note.

Any accidental written *above* the sign alters the higher note of the turn. Any accidental written *below* the sign alters the lower note. Otherwise, only notes of the diatonic scale are used.

In the Mozart Sonata Köchel 279, a turn occurs over a quaver note.

 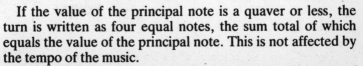

If the value of the principal note is a quaver or less, the turn is written as four equal notes, the sum total of which equals the value of the principal note. This is not affected by the tempo of the music.

If the principal note is a crotchet or longer, the value of the notes of the turn depends upon the tempo of the music. At a slow tempo (less than Allegretto) the turn is a triplet of demisemiquavers joined to a longer note to make up the value of the principal note. At a fast tempo (Allegretto or faster) the turn is four semiquavers plus any necessary note value to make up the worth of the principal note.

If the principal note is a dotted or doubly dotted note the turn is still written according to the general guidance rules stated above. The value of the dot is simply added as a tied note.

There is one exception to what we have learned so far. This is when the principal note is followed by a rest – then, regardless of tempo, a triplet is used.

The *inverted turn*, shown ∿ or ⌇ , is written according to the rules we have learned but the notes are:

(i)   lower note;
(ii)   principal note;
(iii)   upper note;
(iv)   principal note.

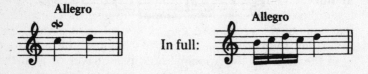

There is an exception to the turn over a note being a four note turn. If the principal note has been preceded by a note one note higher or lower, the complete turn will be a five note one, starting on the principal note.

In full:

At a slow tempo, when the principal note is a quaver or less, make the five notes of the turn each a quarter the value of the principal note. To make these five notes equal the value of the principal note it is necessary to make the first three notes a triplet – three notes in the time of two. When the principal note is a crotchet or longer, the turn is five semiquavers (the first three of which are written as a triplet), the last being tied, if necessary, to a note or notes to make up the value of the principal note.

At Allegretto or faster with a principal note of a quaver or less, write a quintolet of whatever value totals the principal note value. When the principal note is a crotchet or longer write a quintolet of semiquavers, if necessary, joined to a longer note to make up the value of the principal note.

The Turn placed between two notes
At a slow speed – less than Allegretto: when the principal note (that immediately before the turn sign) is undotted and is a crotchet or less, the first note of the turn should be half the value of the principal note, and the value of each of the remaining four notes should be an eighth of the principal note value.

In full:

At a fast speed – Allegretto or more: when the principal note is undotted and the value is a crotchet or less, write the turn as a quintolet (five notes in the time of four of the same kind) – each note a quarter value of the principal note.

In full:

Longer principal notes: with an undotted principal note value of longer than a crotchet, decide how short the last four notes can equally be made (use semiquavers if the tempo is fast and demisemiquavers if slow) and give the remaining value to the first note.

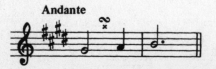

In full:

Dotted principal notes: when the principal note is a dotted note, we must take into consideration whether full or part beats are contained in the ornament.

If the principal note is just one full beat give the first note the value of the undotted portion, the other four notes taking the value of the dot.

In full:

If the principal note is two, three or more full beats, write as for one full beat but tie the additional value before the turn.

In full:

When the principal note contains part of a beat divide the beat into three parts. First and last note each take a third of the value of the beat and the middle section is written as a triplet.

In full:

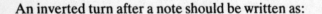

An inverted turn after a note should be written as:

   (i)   the principal note;
  (ii)   the lower note;
 (iii) the principal note;
 (iv) the upper note;
  (v)   the principal note.

The note values obey the various rules already explained.

The Slide

As its name implies, this ornament consists of a slide upwards or downwards between two notes, usually a third or fourth apart. It is shown by tiny notes between normal sized notes. The note values given to the ornament are as for the mordent:

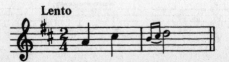

In full   

One occasionally meets a double appoggiatura (two small notes written as for a normal appoggiatura), as in the following example. The double appoggiatura should be treated exactly as the mordent.

In full: 

When either the slide or the double appoggiatura are joined to the trill, they should be incorporated with the same note values as the trill.

Length of Ornaments

Some ornaments vary according to the tempo indication. When there is no such indication, the manner of performance in a piece will depend on the style and conventions of the era of its composition.

QUESTIONS

1. (a) Why is ornamentation used in music?
   (b) How did early singers and instrumentalists create ornaments?
   (c) Are the ornaments ever written out in full by composers?

2. (a) In what value notation should the appoggiatura be written?

(b) What value is given to an appoggiatura written before a crotchet in $\frac{4}{4}$ time?

(c) What value is given to an appoggiatura written before a minim in $\frac{3}{4}$ time?

(d) Write the following in full:

(i)

(ii)

3. (a) What value does the appoggiatura take when written immediately before a dotted note?

(b) Write the following in full:

(i)

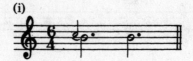

(ii)

(iii)

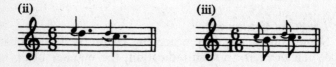

4. (a) What value does the appoggiatura take when immediately before a tied note?

(b) Write the following in full:

(i)

(ii)

(iii)

5. (a) How is an appoggiatura written when it immediately precedes a chord?
   (b) Write out the following as they should be played:

(i)   (ii)   (iii)

6. (a) What is an acciaccatura? Write one.
   (b) What is the origin of 'acciaccatura'?
   (c) How is the acciaccatura performed – on, before or after the beat?
   (d) What effect does the acciaccatura have on the principal note?

7. (a) What value do we give, normally, to the acciaccatura when writing it in full?
   (b) Write the following in full:

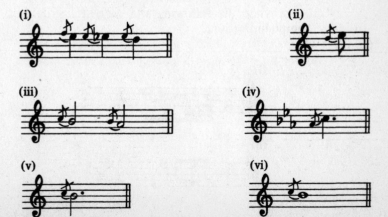

8. (a) What is the difference in appearance between the acciaccatura and the appoggiatura?

   (b) In what other way does the appoggiatura differ from the acciaccatura?

9. (a) What is the sign and what are the notes of an upper mordent?

   (b) What is the sign and what are the notes of a lower mordent?

10. (a) With tempo slower than allegro, how do we write the mordent in full?

    (b) How do we write the mordent in full with tempo allegro or quicker?

    (c) Write the following in full:

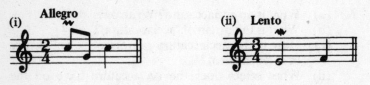

    (d) Abbreviate the following and suggest a suitable tempo indication:

11. (a) What is a double mordent?
     (b) Write signs to show an upper double mordent and a lower double mordent.
     (c) Write the following in full:

12. (a) How does a key signature affect the notes of a mordent?
     (b) How and why would the upper or lower note of an upper or lower mordent be chromatically altered?

13. (a) What is the other name for a trill?
     (b) Of what does a trill consist?
     (c) How is a trill performed?
     (d) How is a trill indicated?

14. (a) On what does the number of alterations in a trill depend?
     (b) What value notes should one use for a tempo of Largo?
     (c) What value notes should one use for a tempo of Vivace?

15. (a) On what note does a trill normally end?
     (b) When does a trill not end on this note?
     (c) Write the following in full:

16. (a) On which note does the trill commence in the music of Mozart and his contemporaries?
    (b) What is special about the number of notes in such a trill?

17. (a) On which note does a trill normally commence?
    (b) What rhythmic peculiarity does this produce and why?
    (c) Where is the triplet written?
    (d) Write out the following in full:

18. (a) If the principal note is preceded by a note of the same pitch, on which note should the trill commence? Why?
    (b) Write out the following in full:

19. (a) How do we treat an acciaccatura when it precedes a trill?

    (b) Write the following in full:

20. (a) If the principal note is prolonged in any way, for how long should the trill continue?

    (b) Write out the following in full:

21. (a) Give two ways in which a composer will indicate that he wants a trill to end with a turn.

    (b) Write out the following in full:

22. (a) How are notes grouped when a turn is added at the end of a trill?

      (b) Should we ever introduce turns not indicated by the composer?

23. (a) What must we remember when writing a turn at the end of a trill on the leading note of a minor key?

      (b) Write the following in full:

Key: G minor

24. (a) With or without a turn, how do we know which note should alternate with the principal note to form our trill?

      (b) How can a composer alter the identity. of the upper note of a trill?

      (c) What does the word modulate mean?

      (d) Write the following in full:

      (e) When can a trill sound like a turn?

25. (a) Write as many variations of the turn as you can remember.

      (b) If a turn has a sharp above, how does this affect the notation?

      (c) If a turn has a flat below, how does this affect the notation?

26. (a) If a turn is written over a note, how many notes should the turn contain?

(b)   Which notes would be played if the turn were over a C?

(c)   Write the following in full:

27.   (a)   With a principal note of a crotchet, upon what does the value of the notes of a turn depend?

(b)   How is the turn on a minim made up at a slow tempo?

(c)   How is the turn on a minim made up at a fast tempo?

(d)   Write the following in full:

28.   Write the following in full:

29.   Write the following in full:

30.   Write the following in full:

(i)   Andante

(ii)   Allegro

31.   Write the following in full:

32.   (a)   How many notes are contained in a turn written after the principal note?

(b)   In such a turn, upon what do the note values depend?

(c)   Write the following in full:

(i)   Adagio

(ii)   Adagio

(iii)   Andante   (iv)   Allegretto

33. (a) If a principal note is longer than a crotchet and is undotted, and the tempo is fast, what note values should be given to the turn?

(b) If a principal note is longer than a crotchet and is undotted, and the tempo is slow, what note values should be given to the turn?

(c) Write the following in full:

34. (a) What must we take into consideration when the principal note of a turn is dotted?

(b) Abbreviate the following:

(i)

(ii)

(iii)

(c) How must we divide the beat when the principal note of a turn contains part of a beat?

(d) Write the following in full:

(i)

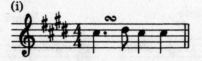

Adagio

(ii)

Allegro assai

(iii)

35. (a) How do we proceed to write a doubly dotted principal note turn?

   (b) Write the following in full:

Adagio

36. Write the following in full:

37. (a) What is a slide?
     (b) How is it shown?
     (c) What note values should be used for the slide?
     (d) Write the following in full:

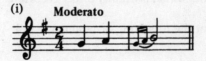

(ii) Allegro

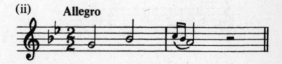

38. (a) What is the sign for a double appoggiatura?
     (b) What value do we give to the notes of this ornament?
     (c) Write the following in full:

(ii)   **Andante**

39.   (a)   How should the slide, or the double appoggia-
            tura, be treated when they precede a trill?

      (b)   Write the following in full:

Andante

40.   In the absence of a tempo indication, by what are we
      guided in deciding how to perform and write out
      ornaments which normally differ according to tempo?

41.   Write out the following ornaments in full:

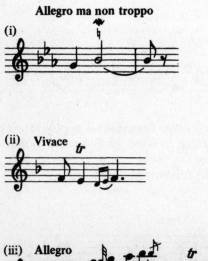

(iv)

(v)   Moderato

(vi)   Allegretto

13

OTHER SCALES AND ABBREVIATIONS USED IN MUSIC

Modes

The major scale of C is simply the white piano notes C, D, E, F, G, A, B, C. If we start on another white note, B for instance, and use only white notes to write our scale we shall produce a different pattern of tones and semitones – B to C is a semitone, C to D a tone, D to E a tone, etc.

Many centuries ago musicians would compose music which fitted into these patterns of tones and semitones. They used scales which they called *modes*. There were seven basic modes:

Aeolian	– TST TSTT	– like the white notes A to A;
Locrian	– STT STTT	– like the white notes B to B;
Ionian	– TTS TTTS	– like the white notes C to C (which is now our major scale);
Dorian	– TST TTST	– like the white notes D to D;
Phrygian	– STT TSTT	– like the white notes E to E;
Lydian	– TTT STTS	– like the white notes F to F;
Mixolydian	– TTS TTST	– like the white notes G to G;

To these were added those which had the same pattern of tones and semitones but which started on a different note. All our major scales are Ionian modes, but starting on different notes. 'Hypo' placed before the name of a mode meant the same pattern of tones and semitones five notes higher. The Hypoaeolian mode, for example, had the same pattern of tones and semitones as the Aeolian (A to A) but started on E. The notes were E, F♯, G, A, B♭, C, D, E.

These altered modes gave rise to the need for the notes F♯ and B♭ and, therefore, also the signs for sharp and flat.

Signs and Abbreviations
The starting of opera and music printing in Italy in the sixteenth century, and the greatest importance of Italy at that time, has left us with many words in Italian which we still use to descibe speed, and other ways of playing our music. Music written in the last two hundred years has, increasingly, used the language of the composer's home country to give these directions.

Dots placed immediately before or after a double bar line indicate repeats.

┇═══════ REPEAT ME ═══════┇

Sometimes composers write the figures 1 and 2 enclosed within lines over the staves at the end of a section of movement.

Beethoven Op. 2 No. 3

The 1 indicates that, at the first playing, that bar is to be played. At the repeat, the bar marked 1 is omitted and bar 2 is substituted. As you will see in the example given, it carries the music on into the next section.

∧ > accents

If we want to show an accent in the music we do not write letters, we use these signs over the notes to be accented.

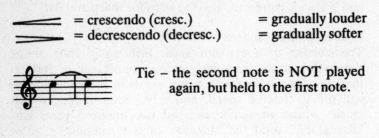

= crescendo (cresc.)   = gradually louder
= decrescendo (decresc.)   = gradually softer

Tie – the second note is NOT played again, but held to the first note.

Legato (slurs) – each note is to follow the one before it without a break in sound. We call this smooth playing *legato*.

Staccato – short and detached. It is shown by dots over, or under, the head of the note. It shortens the note by half.

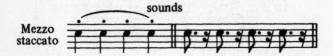

Sometimes, staccato is too short to indicate the intentions of a composer, in which case, he uses the staccato dots, but covers the notes with a legato slur. This is called *mezzo*, or half, staccato. It shortens the note by one quarter.

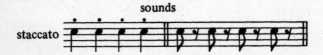

Staccatissimo – shorter than staccato and is shown by a small triangular shape or a vertical line over or under the note(s). It shortens the value of the note by three quarters.

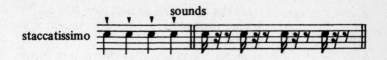

When a composer wants to make a single note mezzo staccato he writes a horizontal line above, or below, the staccato dot.

⌢ or ⌣   Pause sign (Italian = fermata) – is used when a note or group of notes must be held for a pause in the music. The sign is written so that the dot is nearest the head of the note.

Sometimes, this pause sign is not written over or under notes but at the end of a piece or section of a piece.

This often means that the performer should wait a few seconds before starting the next section or repeat. In piano music it is sometimes meant to tell the pianist to keep his hands over the keys for a few seconds at the end of the music so as not to disturb, by moving too quickly, the effect he has created by his playing.

8 – – – – – – – ⌐
       or
8va – – – – – ⌐   = over the notes this means play one octave
                           higher than written. May also appear with
                           a solid line.

8 – – – – – – – – ⌐   = if under the notes, play one octave lower
       or   than written.
8va – – – – – ⌐   The vertical line indicates when to stop.

% or **//**   = repeat of the previous bar

      /   = often used to indicate repeat of previous
                           notes in the same bar

Folksong

is played

m.d. (French: main droite)   = right hand
m.g. (French: main gauche)   = left hand

$\widehat{2}$	Duplet	$\widehat{3}$	Triplet
$\widehat{4}$	Quadruplet	$\widehat{5}$	Quintolet
$\widehat{6}$	Sextolet	$\widehat{7}$	Septolet

pp   = pianissimo = very soft
p   = piano   = soft
mp   = mezzo piano = rather soft, moderately soft
mf   = mezzo forte = rather loud, moderately loud
f   = forte   = loud
ff   = fortissimo = very loud
∧ or > = an accent = a sudden stress in tone on that note or chord
fz   = forzando = a sudden forcing of sound
sfz   = sforzando = a sudden forcing of the tone
accel. = accelerando = gradually faster
cresc. = crescendo = gradually louder
dim.   = diminuendo = gradually softer
Ped.   = Pedal   = use the right (sustaining) pedal of the piano. The depression and release are often shown by lines, thus: ⌐⎯⎯⎯⎯⎯⎯⌐ or Ped . . . . *
rall.   = rallentando = becoming gradually slower
rit.   = ritardando = becoming gradually slower
D.C.   = Da Capo = repeat from the beginning
Fine   = the end. Da Capo al Fine – repeat from the beginning to the word Fine
segno = a sign   = usually such a sign 𝄋 and used together with either the words Dal (meaning 'from') or Al (meaning 'to'): so the direction is from, or to, the sign.

arpeggio – this is usually shown by a wavy line printed vertically before the notes to be played as an arpeggio. The effect is that, beginning on the beat, one plays each note from lowest to highest, one after the other. Here is an example of its use:

Sometimes a composer will not use a wavy line to indicate his wish for an arpeggio, but will write tiny notes before the chord. This is treated exactly as described above, both in playing and, if necessary, in writing out the arpeggio in full.

Beethoven Op. 10 No. 1 Sonata 3rd Mvt

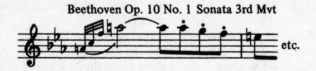

played . . .

tremolo – the Italian word for trembling. On a stringed instrument played with a bow it refers to the technique of rapid repetitions of the same tone by an up and down movement of the bow. On fixed pitch instruments, such as the piano, one makes tremolo by quick alternation between two notes. The two notes to be played are each written the full value of the bar. Between the notes are written tails the equivalent in value to the amount of repetitions intended.

Here, the two notes to be played – A and D – are each the full value of the bar, each a minim. Between the notes are written semiquaver tails which show the amount of repetitions intended, valued according to the time signature which is two crotchet beats. There are eight semiquavers in a bar of $\frac{2}{4}$ time so, in the above example there must be eight notes to be alternated. They must be shown in groups of crotchets because the time signature is a crotchet beat.

One can also write an abbreviation to show the repetitions of single notes of the same pitch. This is done by writing a note equal to the value of the repeats intended and showing the value of the repetitions by tail, as below.

Enharmonic change – a change in name only. For instance, B can be called C♭, or can be called A✖; but these names are only enharmonic changes of name. The pitch remains that of note B.

C enharmonic changes are B♯ and D♭♭ .

D enharmonic changes are C✖ and E♭♭ ;

and so on throughout the whole octave of the scale.

This device is useful to composers when they wish to modulate from one key to another. They can pivot on one note, changing the name of that note to the equivalent in the new key. See how the E♭ below becomes a D♯ .

Musical Terms

The following terms should be understood and memorised:

adagietto	= rather leisurely
adagio	= slow
ad libitum	= at the performer's pleasure
affrettando	= pressing onward, hurrying the speed
allargando	= slower and broader
allegramente	= quickly, cheerfully
allegretto	= rather fast, but not so fast as allegro
allegro	= fast
andante	= walking pace. Indicates an easy pace.
andantino	= at a moderate pace, faster than andante
a piacere	= at the performer's pleasure
a tempo	= back to the original time (usually used after some alteration of tempo to indicate a return to the original or normal time)

ben	= well
bis	= twice. Sometimes when only one or two bars are to be repeated, an encore of them is thus indicated.
calando	= softer and slower
calcando	= hurrying the time
cantabile	= in a singing manner
celere	= quick, nimble
con	= with – usually part of a direction:
	con anima = with soul
	con fuoco = with fire
	con tenerazza = with tenderness
diluendo	= dying away
dolce	= sweetly
doppio tempo	= twice as fast as the preceding movement
doppio movimento	= twice as fast as the preceding movement
giusto	= exact, strict (tempo giusto = in strict time)
grave	= solemn and slow
incalzando	= quicker and louder
largamente	= broadly, massively
larghetto	= rather broadly
largo	= broadly
larghissimo	= very broad
lentamente	= rather slowly
lento	= slow
l'istesso tempo	= same speed as the preceding movement
mancando	= failing or waning in tone
moderato	= moderately fast
meno	= less – usually part of a direction:
	meno allegro – less quickly
	meno mosso – less movement
	meno forte – less loudly
metronome	= a clockwork instrument invented by a man called Mälzel in 1816 for the purpose of helping to keep exact time.
morendo	= dying away

perdendosi	=	losing itself, dying away
pesante	=	heavily, ponderous
più	=	more – usually part of an indication:
		più lento – more slowly
		più piano – more softly
		più mosso – more movement
poco a poco	=	little by little
presto	=	very fast
prestissimo	=	as fast as possible
prestissamente	=	as fast as possible
raddolcendo	=	gradually softer
rinforzando	=	strengthening the tone
ritenuto	=	held back
scemando	=	diminishing in power
senza	=	without
senza sordini	=	without mutes (string or bass players)
		without dampers on the piano
slargando	=	broadening
slentando	=	gradually slower
smorzando	=	extinguishing the tone
stretto	=	pressing onward, hurrying the speed
stringendo	=	gradually faster, hurrying the speed
tempo ordinario	=	ordinary speed
tempo commodo	=	at a convenient speed
tempo giusto	=	in strict or exact time
tempo primo	=	same speed as at first
tosto	=	quickly, rapidly
troppo	=	too much
veloce	=	swiftly
vivace	=	lively
vivacemente	=	rather lively
vivacissimo	=	extremely lively

Foreign Names of the Notes

Composers sometimes use, in the titles of their piece, the key of the music (for example: Bach 'Toccata, Adagio und Fuge in C dur' BWV 564). Of course, they write in their own language.

It would be well to learn the following. Notice the Germans call B♭ – B, and B♮ – H. This fact enabled composers to use as a theme for some works the notes B♭, A, C, B, the German letters of which spell BACH.

English	German	Italian
A♭	As	La bemolle
A	A	La
A♯	Ais	La diesis
B♭	B	Si bemolle
B	H	Si
B♯	His	Si diesis
C♭	Ces	Do bemolle
C	C	Do
C♯	Cis	Do diesis
D♭	Des	Re bemolle
D	D	Re
D♯	Dis	Re diesis
E♭	Es	Mi bemolle
E	E	Mi
E♯	Eis	Mi diesis
F♭	Fes	Fa bemolle
F	F	Fa
F♯	Fis	Fa diesis
G♭	Ges	Sol bemolle
G	G	Sol
G♯	Gis	Sol diesis

French is the same as Italian except that Do is Ut, bemolle is written bémol and diesis is written diese.

The words major and minor in the different languages should be known. They are:

English	German	Italian	French
Major	Dur	Maggiore	Majeur
Minor	Moll	Minore	Mineur

Here are some more Italian words we use to show ways of playing music. A lot of music has been written by German composers, who have used their own language to give these directions. Therefore, we have given the German equivalent of each word.

Italian	English	German
affeto	affectionate	gemütvoll
affettuoso	affectionate	gemütvoll
agitato	agitatedly	aufgeregt
allegretto	rather fast	ziemlich lebhaft
amabile	amiably	liebenswürdig
amaroso	amorously, tenderly	lieblich
animato	animatedly	belebt
appassionato	passionately	leidenschaftlich
arpeggio	harp like	arpeggio
assai	very	sehr
attacca	go on immediately	weitergehen
brillante	brilliantly	glänzend
brio (con)	with spirit	lebhaftigkeit (mit)
calmato	calmly	beruhigt
capriccio	whim	laune
coda	tailpiece (the end part)	schluss
con	with	mit
corda, una	one string (use left piano pedal)	mit einer saite
deciso	decisively	entschieden
delicato	delicately	fein, zart
distinto	distinctly	deutlich
dolore (con)	with grief	schmerzlich
doloroso	with grief	schmerzlich
doppio	double	doppelt
energico	energetically	energisch
eroica	heroic	heldenhaft
espressivo	with expression	mit ausdruck
espressione (con)	with expression	mit ausdruck
feroce	fiercely	wild
fine	the end	Ende
forza (con)	with force	stark, laut
funebre	funereal, sad	trauernd
furioso	furiously	wütend
giocoso	gaily, merrily	speilend, scherzend
grandioso	grandly	grossartig
impetuoso	impetuously	wild

Italian	English	German
incalzando	quicker and louder	jagend
innocente	innocently	unschuldig
legato	smoothly	gebunden
legatissimo	very smoothly	sehr gebunden
leggiero	lightly	leicht
lento	slow	langsam
loco	at original pitch	am platze
lusingando	coaxingly	einschmeichelnd
ma	but	aber
maestoso	majestically	majestätisch
marcato	marked	betont
marcia	march	marsch
martellato	hammered	gehämmert
marziale	martial, warlike	kriegerisch
mesto	sadly	traurig
misterioso	mysterious	geheimnisvoll
mezzo	half	halb
non	not	nicht
Ongarese	Hungarian	Ungarisch
ossia	or	oder
ottave	octave	oktave
parlando	speakingly	sprechend
passione	passionately	leidenschaft
piacevole	pleasantly	anmutig
quasi	in the style of	gleichwie
risoluto	resolute, bold	entschlossen
risvegliato	very animated	frisch
semplice	simply	einfach
sempre	always	immer
sopra	over or above	oben, uber
sotto	under	unten
strepitoso	boisterously	lärmend
subito	suddenly	plötzlich
teneramente	tenderly	zart
tenerezza	tenderly	zart
tenuto	held	ausgehalten
tranquillo	tranquilly	ruhig
tre	three	drei
trionfante	triumphantly	triumphierend
troppo	too much	zu viel

Italian	English	German
un (uno, una)	one	ein
vigoroso	vigorously	energisch
voce	voice	stimme

Una Corda is a direction to a pianist to use the left pedal. On a grand piano this moves the keyboard so that the hammers do not hit all the strings. Today two strings, instead of three (Tre Corde), are hit. Originally one string (Una Corda) would be hit. The effect is to make the sound softer. This is achieved in an upright piano by altering the distance the hammer travels.

Some French composers have used indications in their own language. The following may be a useful list to know.

anime	lively
au mouvement	in time
calme	calm
cédez	hold back (ritenuto)
doucement	sweetly
doux	gentle, sweet
en aimant	in animated manner
en dehors	prominent
en retenant	held back
et	and
expressif	expressively
folatre	playfully
jusqu' à la fin	until the end
léger	lightly
lentement	slowly
lointain	distant
lourdement	heavily
modéré	moderately
moins	less
mouvement	tempo, pace
murmuré	to murmur
peu à peu	little by little
plus	more
retenu	holding back
sans rigueur	without rigidity
souple	soft, supple

très	very
triste	sad
vif	lively
vite	quick

QUESTIONS

1. (a) What name do we use to describe the other patterns of tones and semitones apart from the major and minor scales?
   (b) List and describe these patterns.

2. (a) By what other name can we describe the major scale?
   (b) What does the word 'Hypo' mean?
   (c) Write out, starting each on a suitable note, the following patterns:
      (i)   TST,TTST
      (ii) TST,TSTT
      (iii) TTS,TTST
   and name each pattern.

3. What is the difference between a tie and a slur?

4. (a) What does staccato mean?
   (b) What does legato mean?
   (c) What does mezzo staccato mean?
   (d) What does staccatissimo mean?
   (e) Write these as they should be played:

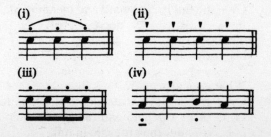

5. (a) What do we call this sign: ⌒?
    (b) What is the Italian word for this sign?
    (c) Where and why would it be used?

6. (a) What do dots immediately before or after a double bar line indicate? Write an example.
    (b) Why is the opening part of a composition often repeated?

7. How do composers sometimes show a variation in the end bar or bars of a section or movement?

8. Write out the following abbreviations in full:

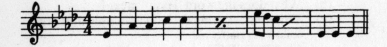

9. (a) Give the Italian for:

little by little	without
slower and broader	very loud
too much	heavily
exact	sweetly
calmly	

(b) Give the English for:

adagio	cantabile	incalzando
meno	Da Capo al Fine	Segno
grave	perdendosi	8 - - - - - - ⌐

(c) Give the full Italian word and meaning of:

ff	sfz -	decresc	rit.
dim.	mp	◁	accel
bis.			

10. (a) What is an arpeggio?
    (b) On a treble stave write the crotchet notes C, E, G, C as an arpeggio and then, after a double bar line, write out the arpeggio in full.
    (c) Write out the following in full:

11. (a) What is the English translation of the word tremolo?

     (b) How does one play a tremolo on an instrument like the violin?

     (c) How does one play a tremolo on the pianoforte?

     (d) Write out the following abbreviations in full:

(e)   Abbreviate the following:

12.   (a)   Write out the following in full:

(i)   (ii)

(b)   Abbreviate the following:

(i)

(ii)

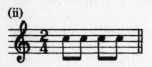

13.   Give the meanings in English for the following:

adagietto	prestissimo	lentamente
raddolcendo	slargando	affretando
smorzando	tempo commodo	doppio movimento
tosto	scemando	veloce
celere	a piacere	mancando
metronome.		

14.   Complete the following:

English	French	German	Italian
			La bemolle
G♯			
	Ut bémol		
		A	
			Re diesis
	La		
D♭			
		His	
A♯			
			Mi bemolle
	Si		
B♭			
		Eis	
			Re

15. Complete the following:

English	French	German	Italian
		Dur	
	Mineur		

16. Complete the following:

English	German	Italian
	gemütvoll	
rather fast		
	liebenswürdig	
amorously, tenderly		
		animato
	leidenschaftlich	
		assai
	weitergehen	
brilliantly		
		con
	deutlich	
the end		
	gebunden	

English	*German*	*Italian*
		leggiero
slow		
	traurig	
		mezzo
speakingly		
		semplice
in the style of		
	immer	
under		
		sopra
	plötzlich	
held		
	drei	
		troppo
one		
	Stimme	

17. (a) What happens when we press down the left
         pedal of a grand piano?
     (b) What was the original meaning of Una Corda?

18. Give the French for:
     until the end   very   lively
     little by little   held back   sweetly
     quick   moderately   lightly
     prominent   slowly   heavily
     sad.

INDEX

RIGHT WAY
PUBLISHING POLICY

HOW WE SELECT TITLES
RIGHT WAY consider carefully every deserving manuscript. Where an author is an authority on his subject but an inexperienced writer, we provide first-class editorial help. The standards we set make sure that every **RIGHT WAY** book is practical, easy to understand, concise, informative and delightful to read. Our specialist artists are skilled at creating simple illustrations which augment the text wherever necessary.

CONSISTENT QUALITY
At every reprint our books are updated where appropriate, giving our authors the opportunity to include new information.

FAST DELIVERY
We sell **RIGHT WAY** books to the best bookshops throughout the world. It may be that your bookseller has run out of stock of a particular title. If so, he can order more from us at any time – we have a fine reputation for "same day" despatch, and we supply any order, however small (even a single copy), to any bookseller who has an account with us. We prefer you to buy from your bookseller, as this reminds him of the strong underlying public demand for **RIGHT WAY** books. Readers who live in remote places, or who are housebound, or whose local bookseller is unco-operative, can order direct from us by post.

FREE
If you would like an up-to-date list of all **RIGHT WAY** titles currently available, send a stamped self-addressed envelope to ELLIOT RIGHT WAY BOOKS, BRIGHTON ROAD,
LOWER KINGSWOOD, TADWORTH, SURREY, KT20 6TD,U.K.
or visit our web site at www.right-way.co.uk